I0447247

Congressional
Research
Service

Moving to a Territorial Income Tax: Options and Challenges

Jane G. Gravelle
Senior Specialist in Economic Policy

July 25, 2012

Congressional Research Service
7-5700
www.crs.gov
R42624

CRS Report for Congress —————————————
Prepared for Members and Committees of Congress

Summary

Among potential tax reforms under discussion by Congress is revising the tax treatment of foreign source income of U.S. multinational corporations. Some business leaders have been urging a movement toward a territorial tax, which would eliminate some U.S. income taxes on active foreign source income. Under a territorial tax, only the country where the income is earned imposes a tax. Territorial proposals include the Grubert-Mutti proposal (included in President Bush's Advisory Panel on Tax Reform proposal in 2005) and, more recently, a draft Ways and Means Committee proposal and a Senate bill, S. 2091. The Fiscal Commission also proposed a territorial tax. Proposals have, however, also been made to increase the taxation of foreign source income, including S. 727, and proposals by President Obama.

Although the United States has a worldwide system that includes foreign earnings in U.S. taxable income, two provisions cause the current system to resemble a territorial tax in that very little tax is collected. Deferral delays paying taxes until income is repatriated (paid as a dividend by the foreign subsidiary to its U.S. parent). When income is repatriated, credits for foreign taxes paid offset the U.S. tax due. Under cross-crediting, unused foreign tax credits from high tax countries or on highly taxed income can be used to offset U.S. tax on income in low tax countries.

Some proponents of a territorial tax urge such a system on the grounds that the current system discourages repatriations. Economic evidence suggests that effect is small, in part because in normal circumstances a large share of income is retained for permanent reinvestment. Amounts held abroad may have increased, however, as firms lobbied for another repatriation holiday (similar to that adopted in 2004) that allowed firms to exempt most dividends from income on a one-time basis. Opponents are concerned about encouraging investment abroad. A territorial tax is generally not viewed as efficient because it favors foreign investment, but that increased outflow of investment is likely to have a small effect relative to the U.S. economy. Artificial shifting of profits into tax havens or low tax countries is a current problem that could be worsened under some territorial tax designs, and proposals have included measures to address this problem.

Proposals also address the transitional issue of the treatment of the existing stock of unrepatriated earnings. The Ways and Means proposal would tax this stock of earnings, but at a lower rate, and use the revenues to offset losses from other parts of the plan, which would lead to a long-run revenue loss. S. 2091 has a similar approach. The Grubert-Mutti proposal does not have a specific transitional tax, but would raise revenue largely due to its disallowance of parent overhead expenses aimed at reducing profit shifting. The other two proposals also contain provisions to address profit shifting.

In addition there are complicated issues in the design of a territorial tax, such as how to treat branches and dividends of firms in which the corporation is only partially owned. A number of issues arise from the ending of foreign tax credits, with perhaps the most significant one being the increased tax on royalties, which are currently subject to tax, have low or no foreign taxes, and would lose the shield of excess credits.

The final section of the report briefly discusses some alternative options, including those in S. 727 and in the Administration proposals. It also discusses hybrid approaches that combine territorial and worldwide systems in a more efficient way, including eliminating the disincentive to repatriate. One such approach is a minimum tax on foreign source income, which is proposed by the President in the context of current rules, but could be combined with a territorial system.

Contents

Tables

Appendixes

Contacts

Introduction

Tax reform is a perennial issue before Congress. One area of increasing attention is the taxation of U.S. companies on the income they earn abroad. Recently, proposals have been made to, in some cases, decrease taxes and in others to increase these taxes.

Businesses leaders have been urging a movement toward a territorial tax, which would generally eliminate U.S. income taxes on active foreign source income. Such a proposal (presumably based on one developed by Grubert and Mutti) was included in the President's Advisory Panel on Tax Reform in 2005,[1] more recently in a draft proposal by Ways and Means Committee Chairman Dave Camp,[2] and in a bill, S. 2091, introduced by Senator Enzi. The National Commission on Fiscal Responsibility and Reform (referred to as the Fiscal Commission) also proposed a territorial tax in general terms.[3]

Proposals have also been made to move in the opposite direction and increase the taxation of foreign source income, including S. 727, introduced by Senators Wyden and Coats, which would use the significant revenues gained to help finance a corporate income tax rate cut. President Obama has included increased taxes on foreign source income in his budget outlines and, more recently, in his framework for business tax reform, as a revenue source for rate reduction.[4]

Because of various features in the current tax system, the U.S. tax system already bears a close resemblance, in terms of revenue collected, to a territorial tax. Tax on the income of foreign subsidiaries is deferred until repatriated (paid as dividends to the U.S. parent) and tax can be avoided by not repatriating income. The system limits credits claimed for foreign taxes paid to U.S. tax on foreign income. The limit, however, is on an overall basis, permitting unused credits from high-tax countries to shield income from low-tax countries, or income that bears little foreign tax, from being taxed in the United States. Because firms have flexibility in timing repatriations, the residual effective tax rate on foreign income is estimated at only 3.3%.[5] Some types of income, such as royalties, are treated more favorably under the current system than they would be under a territorial tax.

---

[1] The President's Advisory Panel on Federal Tax Reform, *Final Report*, November 1, 2005, at http://govinfo.library.unt.edu/taxreformpanel/final-report/index.html. The Grubert-Mutti proposal was the territorial proposal under discussion for a number of years. It is outlined in Harry Grubert and John Mutti, Taxing *International Business Income Dividend Exemption Versus the Current System* (Washington, DC, AEI Press, 2001). It is discussed in further detail in Rosanne Altshuler and Harry Grubert, "Where Will They Go if We Go Territorial? Dividend Exemption and the Location Decisions of U.S. Multinational Corporations," *National Tax Journal* (December 2001), pp. 787-809. Because the current U.S. tax system collects little revenue, and because of features of the Grubert-Mutti proposal to allocate parent company deductions, this proposal would raise revenue.

[2] See various discussions and drafts at the Ways and Means Committee website, at http://waysandmeans.house.gov/taxreform/.

[3] The National Commission on Fiscal Responsibility and Reform, *The Moment of Truth*, at http://www.fiscalcommission.gov/sites/fiscalcommission.gov/files/documents/TheMomentofTruth12_1_2010.pdf.

[4] *The President's Framework for Business Tax Reform A Joint Report by the White House and the Department of the Treasury*, February 2012, at http://www.treasury.gov/resource-center/tax-policy/Documents/The-Presidents-Framework-for-Business-Tax-Reform-02-22-2012.pdf.

[5] Melissa Costa and Jennifer Gravelle, "Taxing Multinational Corporations: Average Tax Rates," presented at a Conference of the American Tax Policy Center, October 2011, and forthcoming in *Tax Law Review* at http://www.americantaxpolicyinstitute.org/pdf/Costa-Gravelle%20paper.pdf.

Economists have traditionally analyzed the foreign tax system in terms of economic efficiency. Economic theory tends to support, on efficiency grounds, a worldwide system in which income from U.S. investment earned abroad is subject to the same tax, or as close to the same tax as possible, as that on domestic investment. It does not support a territorial tax, and most proposals in the past were to move closer to an effective worldwide tax (see **Appendix**). At the same time, if such a change is not feasible, another question becomes whether moving to an explicit territorial tax would be better or worse than the present system. The fundamental issues are

- the effects on disincentives to repatriate income,

- to what extent the revision will divert investment from the United States,

- the effects on artificial profit shifting,

- transition issues,

- administrative and compliance considerations, and

- the revenue consequences.

There is no single blueprint for a territorial tax and the answers to these questions depend, to some extent, on specific design choices.

This report first explains how the international tax system works and describes the magnitude and distribution of foreign source income and taxes. The report then focuses on alternative features of a territorial tax and their consequences. It also contains, in a final section, a brief discussion of options that move in the opposite direction and other alternatives that do not fit into either the territorial or worldwide approach (such as current taxation of foreign source income but at a lower rate).[6]

How the International Tax System Works

The current U.S. tax system is a hybrid. It has some elements of a residence-based or worldwide tax, where income of a country's firms is taxed regardless of its location. It also has some elements of a source based or territorial tax, where all income earned within a country is taxed only by that country regardless of the nationality of the firms. The provisions that introduce territorial features are deferral and cross-crediting. There are a number of complex interactions that will affect both the design of a territorial or other tax revision and the consequences of those changes.

Deferral

Deferral allows a firm to delay taxation of its earnings in foreign subsidiaries until the income is paid as a dividend to the U.S. parent company. Although a territorial tax is often focused on exempting foreign source income that under current law is taxed when repatriated, there are four basic categories of foreign source income, three of which are not eligible for deferral. They are

---

[6] Fundamental economic issues are discussed in CRS Report RL34115, *Reform of U.S. International Taxation Alternatives*, by Jane G. Gravelle.

profits of foreign incorporated subsidiaries; current payment income, such as royalties and interest payments; branch income; and Subpart F income.

Profits of Foreign Incorporated Subsidiaries

U.S. multinationals are not currently taxed on the profits of their subsidiaries incorporated abroad (except for "Subpart F Income" discussed below). Rather they defer payment of taxes until the income is received by the parent as a dividend (repatriated). U.S. tax is then due on the dividend and, because the dividend is after foreign tax, an additional amount (called a gross-up) is added to taxable income to reflect the foreign taxes paid and place the income on a pre-tax basis.[7] A foreign tax credit is then allowed against this U.S. tax.

Current Payment Income

Current payment income is income that is received as a direct payment, such as royalties and interest. It is taxed currently. This income is usually deductible as an expense in the foreign country and, indeed, may not constitute true foreign source income, at least in the case of royalties that could be viewed as more like export income.

Branch Income

Branch income is income from operations that are carried out without a separately incorporated foreign subsidiary. Income of operations organized as foreign branches rather than as separately incorporated subsidiaries is also taxed currently. For tax purposes, branch gross income and deductions are combined with parent income just as if the operation were taking place in the United States. Although branch income is not eligible for deferral, it can be a beneficial form of organization in some cases. If a firm is experiencing a loss, which may be the case with start-ups or mineral or exploration companies, the losses can only reduce U.S. income if the operation is in branch form. In some cases, dividends may attract an additional withholding tax, although for most trading partners these taxes are eliminated or minimized through tax treaties. Non-tax reasons may also cause a firm to choose the branch form; this form, for example, may be particularly beneficial for financial firms in which the branch operation is backed by the assets of the worldwide firm.

Subpart F Income

Subpart F income, named after the section of the Internal Revenue Code that imposes the rules, is income that can easily be shifted to low tax jurisdictions. Subpart F income includes passive income, such as interest and dividends, and certain sales and service income flowing between

---

[7] This discussion generally refers to foreign subsidiaries that are sometimes wholly owned and sometimes partially owned by a U.S. parent. The tax law defines a controlled foreign subsidiary or a controlled foreign corporation (CFC) as one in which the U.S. firm has a 10% share and 50% of the shares are owned by five or fewer 10% U.S. shareholders. A corporation in which a U.S. firm owns a 10% share but 50% is not owned by five or fewer 10% shareholders is called a non controlled Section 902 corporation or a 10/50 corporation. Smaller share ownership is portfolio investment. New data from the Internal Revenue Service reports dividends from firms that are less that 20% owned, more than 20% owned and wholly owned at 7%, 65%, and 27%, although any of these firms could potentially be CFC's and the payout ratios may differ. Filled in 1120 form at http://www.irs.gov/pub/irs-soi/08colinecount.pdf.

related parties (called foreign base company income). This income is taxed currently. Subpart F has been made less effective in recent years because of check-the-box rules that allow flexibility in choosing whether to recognize related firms as separate entities.[8] There are also specific exceptions to Subpart F rules that allow for income from active financing and insurance operations that might otherwise fall under Subpart F to be deferred. These provisions are currently part of the "extenders," provisions that are enacted with an expiration date but that are generally extended periodically. The extenders have currently expired after 2011, although some or all of them they may be extended retroactively. Also among the extenders is a look-through rule that has a similar effect to check-the-box through legislative rather than regulatory rules.[9]

Cross-Crediting

Cross-crediting is a phenomenon that occurs when credits for taxes paid to one country can be used to offset U.S. tax due on income earned in a second country. Cross-crediting occurs because countries generally tax all income arising within their borders from both foreign and domestic firms. The U.S. system allows a credit against U.S. tax due on foreign source income currently taxed for foreign income taxes. This foreign tax credit is designed to prevent double taxation of income earned by foreign subsidiaries of U.S. corporations from facing a combined U.S. and foreign tax in excess of the U.S. tax due if the income was earned in the United States. In addition to cross-crediting across countries, cross-crediting can occur within a country if some income is subject to high tax rates and some is subject to lower tax rates.

If the foreign tax credit had no limit, a worldwide system with current taxation and a foreign tax credit would produce the same result, for firms, as a residence based tax, because the tax effectively applying would be the tax of the country of residence. Firms in countries with a higher rate than the U.S. rate would get a refund for the excess tax, and firms in countries with a lower rate than the U.S. rate would pay the difference. To protect the nation's treasury from excessively high foreign taxes causing excessive revenue losses, however, the credit is limited to the U.S. tax that would be due on the foreign source income. If applied on a country-by-country and income-by-income basis, this rule would result in higher taxes paid on incomes and/or in countries where foreign taxes are higher than U.S. taxes. The rule would also result in total taxes paid equal to the U.S. tax when foreign taxes are lower. If applied overall or in a way that can combine income subject to high taxes with income subject to low taxes, unused credits in high-tax countries (or associated with highly taxed income) can be used to offset U.S. tax due in low-tax countries or income subject to low taxes. This mechanism is called cross-crediting.

Cross-crediting is important to consider when evaluating international tax changes, including the move to a territorial tax, because cross-crediting would largely disappear with the disappearance of foreign tax credits associated with exempted income. Excess credits could no longer shield certain direct active income such as royalties from U.S. taxes.

---

[8] Check-the-box allows a firm, including a subsidiary of a U.S. firm, to choose to disregard (not recognize) its own subsidiary as a separate entity and consolidate that income with the parent (higher tier subsidiary) firm. For example, if a U.S. parent's subsidiary in a low-tax country lends money to its own subsidiary in a high-tax county (with deductions for interest paid), the interest income received by the low-tax subsidiary would normally be taxed as Subpart F income even if this income is not repatriated to the U.S. parent. Check-the-box allows the high-tax subsidiary to be disregarded for tax purposes so that no interest income appears.

[9] See David R. Sicular, "The New Look-Through Rule: W(h)ither Subpart F?" *Tax Notes*, April 23, 2007, pp. 349-378 for a discussion of this provision.

A variety of tax rules can affect the degree and nature of cross-crediting: separating income and credits into baskets with cross-crediting only allowed within the basket; characterizing certain royalty and export income as foreign source; restricting the use of excess credits generated from oil and gas extraction; and interest and other expense allocation rules. In addition, a provision that effectively allowed claiming of foreign tax credits when the associated income was not subjected to U.S. tax, termed foreign tax credit splitting, may have affected past practices and data. This provision was restricted in 2010.

Firms whose foreign tax payments are larger than those permitted to be credited under the foreign tax credit limit rules are said to be in an excess credit position. Firms whose tax payments are smaller are in an excess limit position.[10]

Foreign Tax Credit Limit Baskets

While the United States has had a variety of limit rules in the past,[11] it currently has an overall limit that allows cross-crediting, separated into two significant baskets based on the type of income: an active or general basket and a passive basket. About 95% of income is in the general basket so there is much scope for cross-crediting.[12] Therefore, companies that have paid taxes higher than the U.S. rate can still (within each basket) offset U.S. taxes on income earned in low-tax countries. Higher tax rates can also offset taxes on income generally taxed at low or no rates; one example is royalties associated with active operations, which fall in the active basket and may be shielded from U.S. tax by excess foreign tax credits. Another is foreign source income from export sales, discussed below under the "Title Passage Rule."

Separate Limit on Oil and Gas

The law also contains separate restrictions on certain other types of income, one of importance, as measured by foreign income affected, being oil and gas extraction income. A separate provision disallows credits paid on oil and gas extraction income in excess of the U.S. tax due, although they can be carried over to future years. This treatment has the effect of placing oil and gas extraction income in a separate basket, because generally this income is subject to high foreign taxes. For example, if the U.S. tax on foreign oil and gas extraction income is 35% and the foreign tax is 50%, the extra 15% credit cannot be used to offset tax on other income. This treatment has the same effect as placing this oil and gas extraction income in a separate basket. If the tax on oil and gas extraction income were lower than the U.S. tax, this income would be eligible to have the additional U.S. tax offset by excess credits on other income because income from oil and gas extraction income is not actually in a different basket.

---

[10] Fewer excess credit firms in recent years also led to transactions designed to generate foreign tax credits, but these have now been limited by regulation. See Steven Schneider, Regulations Address Foreign Tax Credit Generator Structures, at http://www.taxlawroundup.com/2011/07/regulations-address-foreign-tax-credit-generator-transactions/.

[11] A per country limit was used in the past at various times, but because it did not have look-through rules, holding companies could be used to accomplish the effects of an overall limit. While an overall credit limit has been used for some time, between 1986 and 2004, the credit was applied within nine different baskets.

[12] Scott Luttrel, "Corporate Foreign Tax Credit, 2007," Internal Revenue Service, *Statistics of Income Bulletin*, 2011, at http://www.irs.gov/pub/irs-soi/11cosumbulcorpforeign.pdf. There are two very small baskets for income from countries sanctioned by the United States and income resourced by treaty, which accounted for less than two-tenths of a percent. Prior to 2007 when there were nine baskets, but the only important difference was a separation of the financial services basket, with 19.7% of income, from the general basket.

Allocation of Deductions

Another feature that may contribute to the generation of excess foreign tax credits is the allocation of overhead and other deductions that are not taken for foreign tax purposes. While many deductions can be traced to a particular source of income, the parent firm's costs for interest, research, and other overhead (e.g. administration) is allocated between domestic and foreign uses for purposes of the foreign tax credit limit. This allocation lowers the amount of foreign source income. Because these reductions in income are not recognized by the foreign jurisdiction, the result could be to generate excess credits, even in countries whose general effective tax rate is actually lower than that of the United States.

These allocations are necessary for determining net income by source. Borrowing is generally done at the parent level. In addition, the interest allocation limits the ability of firms who are in the excess credit position to avoid U.S. tax by borrowing in the United States rather than in low-tax countries where the deduction is less valuable.

The rule, however, has some imperfections. Foreign subsidiaries may also have overhead costs, particularly interest, which are not recognized in income because dividends are received net of deductions. In 2004, a revision that would have allowed elective allocation of worldwide interest, was adopted but did not go into effect immediately. This elective worldwide interest allocation rule has been delayed on several occasions; currently it is scheduled to take place in 2021.

Title Passage Rule

There is a special rule called the title passage rule (or the inventory sales source exception rule) that allows half of manufacturing export income (and all of sales of inventory) to be sourced as income in the country in which the title passes. Because this title passage can be arranged in foreign countries, this income is foreign source income and thus eligible for cross-crediting. This provision is effectively an export subsidy for firms with excess foreign tax credits. The title passage rule is important in considering a territorial tax because cross-crediting, at least for active income, would, in theory, disappear. Export income, as well as royalties, would be subject to higher tax rates in some cases with elimination of foreign tax credits.

Foreign Tax Credit Splitting (Now Restricted)

Prior to 2010, there was also a possibility of claiming foreign tax credits for income that had not actually been subject to tax due to differing rules across countries as to entity status.[13] P.L. 111-226 disallowed any consideration of a foreign tax credit unless the underlying income was reported. Although this provision was estimated to gain relatively little revenue (about $0.4 billion annually),[14] it is hard to be certain how prevalent these activities were. These arrangements

---

[13] These treatments were referred to as reverse hybrids, and they occurred when, from the U.S. perspective, the subsidiary has its own subsidiary where profits can be deferred, but from the foreign perspective the subsidiary and its own subsidiary are the same firm. The top tier subsidiary thus confronts a foreign tax it is liable for and which could be claimed as a credit even though the income is not reported because it is eligible for deferral. It is the reverse of the check the box arrangement.

[14] This provision was adopted in the P.L. 111-226. See Joint Committee on Taxation, *General Explanation Of Tax Legislation Enacted In The 111th Congress*, JCS-2-11, March 24, 2011, for the revenue estimate for this provision and for several other revisions of the foreign tax credit to address abuses. See also CRS Report R40623, *Tax Havens International Tax Avoidance and Evasion*, by Jane G. Gravelle.

---

may affect the data currently available by increasing the ability of firms to offset, for example, royalties with excess credits.

The Magnitude and Distribution of Foreign Source Income and Taxes, Actual and Potential

Before discussing the issues and consequences of reforms, it is useful to get a "lay of the land." How important are the various sources of foreign income, how much tax do they generate currently, and how much might they generate with various reforms? Because individual tax return data are not available, this issue can only be explored by combining aggregate data available and various analyses that have been done by researchers with access to tax returns. This section discusses the current sources of foreign income, the potential magnitude of foreign income not reported, the sources of tax liability, and the potential size of foregone taxes due to deferral and cross-crediting.

Current Sources of Realized Foreign Income

Table 1 shows the distribution of foreign source income by type for firms claiming and receiving foreign tax credits for 2007 and 2008, to the extent that sources can be identified. This data set should capture most of foreign source income reported by U.S. multinationals on their tax return (i.e., not deferred). (Although some data are available for 2009, these data may be skewed because of the economic slowdown that spread abroad). Total foreign source net income was $392.5 billion in 2007 and $413.4 billion in 2008. In the data, oil and gas extraction income is reported separately, so that dividends do not include that income.

Table 1. Distribution of Foreign Source Income Realized in the United States by Type, 2007 and 2008

Type of Income	Share of Taxable Income, 2007 (%)	Share of Taxable Income, 2008 (%)
Dividend Payments	19.2	22.2
Includable Income (Subpart F)	16.6	16.5
Deemed Taxes (Gross Up)	12.9	16.9
Export Income	3.7	3.5
Royalties, and License Payments (Gross)	26.0	25.7
IC-DISC	2.3	0.0
Other	19.4	15.2

Source: Statistics of Income, International Statistics, Returns With Foreign Tax Credits, http://www.irs.gov/taxstats/bustaxstats/article/0,,id=210069,00.html; Royalties and License Payments adjusted to eliminate rents based on data from Bureau of Economic Analysis, Trade in Services, 1999-2010, http://www.bea.gov/scb/pdf/2011/07%20July/0711_itaq-tables.pdf. Foreign taxes withheld as reported in the IRS data are added to royalties. Total taxable income for royalties from the Commerce Department data was increased by withholding taxes of approximately $4 billion.

Notes: Newly provided data for 2008 and 2009 separate the deemed tax gross up; for 2008, 73% of these taxes were associated with dividend payments and the remainder with Subpart F. See Internal Revenue Service http://www.irs.gov/pub/irs-soi/08co inecount.pdf.

Note that the third item in the table is related to the first two. Because dividends and Subpart F income are on an after-tax basis, the dividends must be increased by the taxes paid for corporate taxpayers electing a foreign tax credit. Most of the deemed paid taxes are probably associated with dividend payments (73% for 2008 when data first because available)[15] because Subpart F income is usually subject to lower foreign taxes. Accordingly, the data suggest an estimate of 30% to 35% of foreign source income that arises from these dividends.

The table also shows that royalties are significant parts of foreign source income, accounting for about a quarter of foreign source income, suggesting that the consequences of changes in the law for this income might be significant.

In **Table 1**, the measure of net income was income net of all deductions (but before adjustments). Some of these deductions were overhead costs that are allocated based on formulas. In **Table 2**, shares are calculated based on income before these allocated deductions. With this approach, it is also possible to calculate the share of interest income and oil and gas extraction income. In **Table 2**, foreign source income before non-allocable deductions is $615.4 billion in 2007 and $614.6 billion in 2008. Non-allocable deductions accounted for 36% of this income in 2007 and 33% in 2008.

**Table 2. Distribution of Realized Foreign Source Income
Before Non-Allocable Deductions, 2007 and 2008**

Type of Income	Share of Taxable Income, 2007 (%)	Share of Taxable Income, 2008 (%)
Dividend Payments	12.2	14.9
Includable Income (Subpart F)	8.3	11.1
Deemed Taxes (Gross Up)	10.6	11.4
Export Income	2.3	2.3
Royalties, and License Payments (Gross)	16.6	17.3
IC-DISC	1.4	0.0
Oil and Gas Extraction Income	10.2	15.9
Service Income	2.8	3.2
Interest	21.3	18.4
Other (rents, other branch income)	14.3	5.3

Source: Statistics of Income, International Statistics, Returns With Foreign Tax Credits, http://www.irs.gov/taxstats/bustaxstats/article/0,,id=210069,00.html; Royalties and License Payments adjusted to eliminate rents based on data from Bureau of Economic Analysis, Trade in Services, 1999-2010, http://www.bea.gov/scb/pdf/2011/07%20July/0711_itaq-tables.pdf. Foreign taxes withheld as reported in the IRS data are added to royalties. Total taxable income for royalties from the Commerce Department data was increased by withholding taxes of approximately $4 billion.

Notes: Newly provided data for 2008 and 2009 separate the deemed tax gross up; for 2008, 73% of these taxes were associated with dividend payments and the remainder with Subpart F. See Internal Revenue Service http://www.irs.gov/pub/irs-soi/08co inecount.pdf.

---

[15] See Internal Revenue Service http://www.irs.gov/pub/irs-soi/08colinecount.pdf.

Dividend payments and their related tax gross ups are smaller as a share (25% to 30%) when pre-tax income is considered. Their true importance probably lies somewhere between the shares in **Table 1** and **Table 2** given the imperfections in allocation rules. Note however, that oil and gas extraction income can arise from a subsidiary and is simply reported separately. Including oil and gas income in dividends would bring the totals back up toward 35% to 40% of income. Oil and gas extraction income, however, has little or no reason not to be repatriated because the taxes due on these earnings are generally larger than the U.S. tax (which is why they are treated separately in a way that effectively results in a separate basket). **Table 2** also shows the importance of interest income in the totals for foreign source income (although a full measure of the importance of interest would require information on income of financial institutions through branches).

Deferred Income

Table 1 and **Table 2** report realized income (direct, repatriated, branch, and Subpart F). Total foreign source income also includes deferred income. How large is this deferred income on an annual basis? Estimates in this section indicate that close to half of foreign source income is subject to U.S. tax, but less than a quarter of active income of foreign subsidiaries of U.S. firms that can be deferred is currently repatriated.

There are no precise data sources to estimate this effect. Based on IRS statistics for controlled foreign corporations, available for 2008, which accounted for $177 billion of distributions out of pre-tax income to U.S. parents (about 78% of the total distributions), total deemed and distributed income was 27% of total pre-tax income. Subpart F income was 12.1% of pre tax income and dividends were 14.7%.[16] As a share of after tax income, dividends were 18.1% of income and Subpart F 14.3% income, for a total of 32.4%. These ratios might be somewhat understated because of the possibility of non-U.S. shareholders, but that is likely to be unimportant.

Commerce Department data (Table 6.16D: Corporate Profits by Industry) reports $511 billion and $582 billion of rest of world corporate profits in 2007 and 2008, on an after-tax basis.[17] Considering distributions after foreign tax in 2007, the ratios are 14.7% for dividends and 12.7% for Subpart F income, for a total of 27.4%. These ratios are 15.7% for dividends, 12.0% for Subpart F, and 27.8% for the total for 2008.

These numbers do not capture deemed taxes. Using IRS data on controlled foreign corporations and based on the ratios of deemed taxes to distributions in **Table 1** (with 73% of deemed taxes associated with active dividends), the share of pre-tax profits including taxes for 2008 was 19.7% for dividends and 14.7% for Subpart F. Because Subpart F is not voluntary, the share of dividends out of pre-tax profits net of Subpart F income is 23%.

A study of the new M-3 form that reconciles tax and book income finds that for firms with positive taxable and book income, 9% of the foreign source income is actively paid as a dividend and 47% is subject to U.S. tax (including royalties and other direct). Dividends as a share of total income are 19%, the same share as in **Table 1**. The ratios would be similar to those above if deemed taxes were included.

---

[16] Internal Revenue Service, Statistics of Income, Controlled Foreign Corporations, at http://www.irs.gov/taxstats/bustaxstats/article/0,,id=96282,00.html. Firms represented in these statistics have a 50% ownership or more.

[17] Department of Commerce, Bureau of Economic Analysis, Table 6.16D, at http://www.bea.gov/international/di1usdop.ht.m.

Overall, it appears that close to half of foreign source income is reported as taxable income in the United States, but less than a quarter of the income over which firms have discretion, active income of foreign subsidiaries, is subject to U.S. tax. Rates of deferral vary significantly by location. For 2008, in the aggregate 33% of after tax income of controlled foreign corporations was distributed, 18% as discretionary dividends and the remaining 15% as Subpart F income. Canadian subsidiaries, however, distributed 44%, with 36% as discretionary payments and the remaining 8% as Subpart F. However, for Switzerland, a significant tax haven country, 19% was paid out, 10% as dividends and the remaining 9% as Subpart F. These shares are not available for 2007, and 2006 is probably not very representative, at least for tax haven countries, because it was immediately after the repatriation holiday enacted in 2004 that permitted a one-time dividend payment with an 85% exclusion.[18]

In determining the consequences of present and proposed systems, it is also important to note the repatriated income is not random. Firms presumably choose to repatriate income that can be most easily shielded by foreign tax credits. Some evidence of this effect can be found in the M-3 study, in which the residual U.S. tax on foreign source income was only 3.3% even though half of income was reported and a significant share was in royalties that had little foreign tax (to be used for credits) attached.

Sources of Tax Liability

To examine this issue, consider the data in **Table 3** on foreign tax credits, which indicate the foreign taxes paid, and credits claimed.

Table 3. Foreign Tax Payments and Credits, 2007 and 2008

Item	2007 ($ billions)	2008 ($ billions)
Current Foreign Taxes Paid	99.1	156.2
Minus Reduction (Largely for Oil and Gas Taxes)	10.3	14.7
Plus Carryover	29.2	49.7
Equals Total Foreign Tax Credits Available	117.9	191.2
Foreign Tax Credit Limit	114.0	122.5
Foreign Tax Credits Claimed	86.5	100.4
Residual U.S. Tax (Limit Minus Claim)	29.5	22.1

Source: Statistics of Income, International Statistics, Returns With Foreign Tax Credits, http://www.irs.gov/taxstats/bustaxstats/article/0,,id=210069,00.html.

Even though a significant share of the income was royalties and other direct income that should have been taxed, the effective U.S. residual tax rate on foreign source income as measured for tax purposes was only 7% in 2007 and 5% in 2008.[19] Moreover, the size of the tax suggests that royalties were being shielded from tax by excess credits. The royalties were $101.9 billion and $106.4 billion. Had they been fully subject to a 35% tax rate the tax on this source of income

---

[18] For 2006 total payments were 25% with 12% as discretionary dividends. The data for Canada were similar, but in Switzerland 16% was paid out in total but only 3% as dividends.

[19] Residual U.S. tax in **Table 3** divided by net income from statistics reported in **Table 1**.

(offset by approximately $4 billion in withholding taxes) would have been around $32 billion and $33 billion respectively, larger than total taxes paid.

The indication that royalties are shielded from tax is reinforced by evidence from 2000 tax returns, which traced the $12.7 billion of U.S. residual taxes to foreign sources.[20] **Table 4** shows the distribution of the shares paid. In 2000, there were nine foreign tax credit limit baskets. Only three accounted for a significant share: passive (4.6% of the total), financial services (21.3% of total), and the residual general limit basket (71.3% of the total).[21] Active dividends in the general basket accounted for only 10.2% of total taxes and dividends in financial services accounted for 2.4%. The largest share was due to royalties, interest, and branch income in the active basket. Financial branch income and financial interest each accounted for 18% so that the financial income basket bore a share of taxes out of proportion to its share of income, presumably in part because interest income was subject to tax. The remainder, 16.5% was due to the passive basket, which was largely composed of Subpart F income.

Table 4. Estimated Sources of Tax Revenue on Foreign Source Income, 2000

Type of Income	Share of Taxes Paid (%)
Dividends Non-Financial Services	10.2
Dividends Financial Services	2.4
Active Royalties, Interest and Export (Non-Financial)	33.9
Financial, Branch Income	18.1
Financial, Interest	18.1
Passive (Largely Subpart F)	16.5

Source: Harry Grubert and Rosanne Altshuler, "Corporate Taxes in the World Economy: Reforming the Taxation of Cross-border Income," in *Fundamental Tax Reform: Issues, Choices, and Implications*, Ed. John W. Diamond and George R. Zodrow, Cambridge, MIT Press, 2008, pp. 326-327.

If current taxes were distributed in the same manner now as they were in 2000, then taxes on active dividends for 2007 would have been responsible for a residual U.S. tax of around one-half of 1% on total foreign source active income potentially paid out as dividends.[22] The combination of selective deferral and cross-crediting appears to have essentially eliminated any U.S. tax on active income of foreign subsidiaries.

The same study that estimated data for **Table 4** estimated that two-thirds of royalties were shielded by tax credits. It is possible, however, that more tax is collected on royalties currently because of the declines in foreign tax rates and the elimination of foreign tax credit splitting.

---

[20] Harry Grubert and Rosanne Altshuler, "Corporate Taxes in the World Economy: Reforming the Taxation of Cross-border Income," in John W. Diamond and George R. Zodrow, eds., *Fundamental Tax Reform Issues, Choices, and Implications* (Cambridge: MIT Press, 2008).

[21] Data on distribution by basket from Scott Luttrell, Corporate Foreign Tax Credit, 2000, Internal Revenue Service, *Statistics of Income*, at http://www.irs.gov/pub/irs-soi/00cftcar.pdf.

[22] Pre-tax income would range from $112 billion for 2007 to $142 billion for 2008 (with deemed tax apportioned 73% on active dividends. 12.6% of the total tax in **Table 3** would result in $3.7 billion in 2007 and $2.8 billion in 2008, for an effective tax rate of 3.3% and 1.6% on dividends received. However, estimates above indicate that only about 23% of dividends are paid out, so that these tax rates need to be multiplied by 0.23, yielding rates of 0.36% to 0.76%.

Current and Potential Tax Collections

To consider a year that should be more normal (i.e., past the effects of a slow recovery from the recession) **Table 5** estimates three components of potential foreign taxes for FY2014: foreign taxes projected to be collected, additional taxes collected as a result of the repeal of deferral, and additional taxes collected if, in addition to repealing deferral, a per country foreign tax credit were imposed. Those provisions taken together should result in a close approximation of a true worldwide system that eliminated deferral and largely eliminates cross-crediting.

Table 5. Current and Potential Tax Collections on Foreign Source Income, FY2014

Provision	Effect on Revenues ($billions)	Share of Current Total U.S. Corporate Tax (%)
Current Tax	32.1	7.5
Gain from Ending Deferral	18.4	4.3
Additional Gain from Per Country Foreign Tax Credit Limit	45.9	10.9
Total Share of All	96.4	22.5
Addendum: Eliminate Title Passage Rule	6.3	1.6
Addendum: Repeal Worldwide Interest Allocation	3.6	0.8

Source: Current Tax extrapolated from 2007 data based on changes in corporate tax revenues. Gain from Ending Deferral and Title Passage Rule from Joint Committee on Taxation, *Estimates Of Federal Tax Expenditures For Fiscal Years 2011-2015*, January 17, 2012, JCS-1-12. Gain from Per Country Foreign Tax Credit Limit from Joint Committee on Taxation estimates at http://wyden.senate.gov/imo/media/doc/Score.pdf; Worldwide interest allocation based on FY2019 cost adjusted to FY2014 based on projected corporate tax revenues; FY2019 cost at Joint Committee on Taxation, *General Explanation Of Tax Legislation Enacted In The 111th Congress*, JCS-2-11, March 24, 2011.

This table shows the importance of cross-crediting, by showing the effects of moving to a per country foreign tax credit limit given deferral is eliminated. Because of this importance, a territorial tax, which would eliminate foreign tax credits, can have consequences beyond the active income it is designed to remove from the U.S. tax base, since excess credits currently shield royalty and export income from U.S. tax.

Table 5 also shows the separate revenue consequences of two other provisions: the title passage rule and the effect of worldwide allocation of foreign source income.

Issues in Considering Territorial Taxation

Several issues arise when considering moving from the present hybrid tax system to a territorial tax: the effect on repatriations, the effect on the location of real investment, the consequences for artificial profit shifting, transition, administrative and compliance issues, and the revenue consequences.

Effect on Repatriations

One criticism of the current system is that while collecting very little revenue from foreign subsidiaries, it nevertheless discourages repatriations. The negative effect of the current system on repatriations is the major economic rationale cited by the Ways and Means Committee's press release proposing a territorial tax.[23] This argument also ties the lower repatriation rates to less investment and fewer jobs in the United States.

Before discussing the potential effects, however, note that the repatriation argument alone is not a sufficient justification for a territorial tax. The tax effect on repatriation could be eliminated by moving in the opposite direction, ending deferral. Or it could be achieved by a variety of hybrid approaches such as taxing a fixed share of profits currently and exempting the remainder, or allowing an exemption combined with a minimum tax that is smaller than the U.S. tax rate. All of these approaches create a system where taxation is not triggered by repatriation.

Would the elimination of the tax triggered by repatriations (which could be achieved by either a territorial tax or elimination of deferral) increase repatriations significantly? And if so, would those increased repatriations result in more investment and jobs in the United States?

Although the projections vary with data source and with shares of pre-tax and after-tax income, estimates in the previous section suggest that about a third of foreign subsidiaries' earnings was repatriated, with discretionary distributions net of Subpart F income around 23%. Does that imply that the remaining two thirds of income (or 77% of income net of Subpart F distributions) would be repatriated? It is unlikely that much of an increase would occur, as discussed below, and even more unlikely that it those repatriations would be translated into investment.

Several considerations suggest that the increase in repatriations would be limited. First, regardless of tax considerations, much of foreign source earnings would be retained abroad to be reinvested in the enterprises there. Historical evidence on corporate rates of return and growth rates in the United States suggest that about 60% of nominal income is typically retained to maintain the real capital stock and allow it to grow normally at a steady state.[24] The remainder, 40%, would be distributed. Thus we might expect, using the estimates above, at best to see an increase of 7% of earnings, or 17% of earnings net of Subpart F income.

Second, these repatriation rates are probably at an unusually low level because they followed the large one time repatriation (generally in 2005) from the temporary repatriation holiday enacted in 2004. Not only had large sums been repatriated to take advantage of a one time tax exemption which reduced the need for repatriations immediately after the holiday, but more might have been retained abroad than usual in anticipation of another holiday.[25] Historical data indicate that

---

[23]Camp Releases International Tax Reform Discussion Draft , October 26, 2011, at http://waysandmeans.house.gov/News/DocumentSingle.aspx?DocumentID=266168.

[24] If the rate of return were 10%, the steady state nominal growth rate were 6% (a typical value reflecting a real growth rate of 3% and an inflation rate of 3%), then the remainder would be paid out as a 4% dividend yield. These are typical historical values in the United States. Thus, in a steady state growth model with these values, 60% of nominal earnings would be retained in any case (and would be retained if taxes did matter), and 40% paid out.

[25] See CRS Report R40178, *Tax Cuts on Repatriation Earnings as Economic Stimulus An Economic Analysis*, by Donald J. Marples and Jane G. Gravelle. Another repatriation holiday was voted on in the Senate in 2009, but not adopted.

---

repatriation rates fell towards the end of the 1990s and continued to be low from 2000 to 2008.[26] Data were provided every other year and did not include 2005, the year most repatriations occurred under the repatriation holiday. Over the period 1968-2008, the average repatriation rate was 40%; for 2000-2008 it was 20%. In addition to the anticipation and aftermath of repatriation holidays, the growth of high-tech and dot.com firms that were expanding rapidly and not initially paying dividends may also have affected these payout ratios.[27] The evidence from tax data is also consistent with studies examining repatriation rates over an earlier period of time using financial data that found rates of around 40%.[28] Since a 40% rate is about the rate that might be expected in a no-tax world, these results suggest that the repatriation tax has had relatively little effect on a permanent basis. If firms came to believe another repatriation holiday or territorial tax were not in store, and the high-tech industries achieved a steady state growth, repatriation rates might rise to more normal levels.

Third, there is direct evidence that shifting to a territorial tax would not have large effects. Some initial evidence indicates that the Japanese shift to a territorial tax increased repatriations in the first year by about 20%.[29] Applied to current realizations rates, it would increase realizations by about 4% of total earnings; compared to the 40% rate it would increase realizations by about 8% of earnings. Since a larger first year effect might be expected, as pent up earnings are returned, such an increase is quite modest. Preliminary results from a study of the UK territorial tax shift, while subject to revision, suggest an increase of 6% of earnings.[30] A statistical study of U.S. affiliates in different countries facing different taxes suggested that repatriations would increase by about 13%, which would be 2.5% to 5% of earnings.[31]

Moreover, some theory and research suggests the effects would be negligible on a permanent basis. Theoretical considerations indicate that the repatriation tax should not matter because firms will eventually have to repatriate earnings. This theory, referred to as the "new view" is related to a similar theory about why domestic firms pay dividends to their individual shareholders even though it triggers a dividend tax. In both cases, the idea is that eventually shareholders will want to receive their dividends in excess of amounts needed for steady state reinvestment and dividends will be paid either currently, or in the future with interest. In either case, the same present value of tax will occur. While this "new view" for dividends paid in the U.S. to its individual shareholders could be rejected on the grounds that firms can return cash to the

---

[26] Data from 1992 to 2008 were from Internal Revenue Service Statistics of Income, Data on Controlled Foreign Corporations, http://www.irs.gov/taxstats/bustaxstats/article/0,,id=97151,00 html. Data from 1968-1992 reported in James R. Hines, Jr., The Case Against Deferral: A Deferential Consideration, *National Tax Journal* ,Vol. 52, September 1999, pp. 385-404.

[27] The evidence does not support the idea that the fall in repatriations was due to check-the-box, which was first announced at the beginning of 1997. Subpart F income did not begin to decline as a share of income until 2004.

[28] Mehir A. Desai, C. Fritz Foley, and James R. Hines, Jr., Dividend Policy Inside the Multinational Firm, *Financial Management,* March 22, 2007, at http://www.thefreelibrary.com/Dividend+policy+inside+the+multinational+firm.-a0167305683.

[29] Testimony of Mr. Gary M. Thomas Before the Committee on Ways & Means, U.S. House of Representatives, Hearing on How Other Countries Have Used Tax Reform To Help Their Companies Compete in the Global Market and Create Jobs, May 24, 2011, at http://www.whitecase.com/files/Uploads/Documents/GThomas-HWM-Testimony-24May2011.pdf.

[30] Peter Egger, Valeria Merlo, Martin Ruf, and Georg Wamser, *The Consequences of the new UK Tax Exemption System Evidence from Micro-level Data,* Working Paper, January 26, 2012.

[31] Mehir A. Desai, C. Fritz Foley, and James R. Hines, Jr., "Repatriation Taxes and Dividend Distortions, " *National Tax Journal,* Vol. 54, December 2001, pp. 829-851.

economy by repurchasing shares, such an option is not available for dividend payments between a multinational affiliate and its parent.

If the theory correctly describes behavior, then one would expect that, regardless of the repatriation tax a similar share of earnings would be paid in dividends with or without a repatriation tax. A large empirical literature has developed to study repatriation behavior, finding a variety of results. For example, some early evidence suggested that repatriation rates are sensitive to tax, but subsequent research showed that it might be due to transitory effects.[32] Evidence that repatriations were more likely from highly taxed subsidiaries (where taxes generated would be offset by foreign tax credits) relative to low taxed ones suggested that taxes have effects on repatriations.[33] However, another study found that the repatriations tax became less important given alternative strategies for returning cash for the United States.[34] These strategies included making passive investments abroad with the parent company borrowing against them, or having low tax subsidiaries make equity investments in high tax subsidiaries which in turn repatriated income with attached foreign tax credits.[35] These strategies would indicate differential repatriation rates exist between high and low tax subsidiaries but they are not necessarily meaningful. Most recently, a study suggested taxes had some effect, but a limited one, on repatriations; this study also showed over a long period of time payout shares of about 40%.[36]

The recent pressure for a repatriation holiday and reports of large amounts of accumulated unrepatriated earnings probably comes largely from firms that have intangible assets, have been growing rapidly abroad and thus retaining earnings for that purpose, and perhaps shifting profits arbitrarily.[37] They may have also been delaying repatriations in anticipation of another holiday. As affairs settle into more of a steady state, there may be a greater need to distribute to pay shareholders, so this phenomenon may be largely transitory.

Even if repatriations increase under a permanent territorial tax, those repatriations may not result in additional investment, but are likely to be paid out as dividends, or substitute for borrowing by the parent company.[38] Job creation is not the primary focus here in any case, as in the long run,

---

[32] See Rosanne Altshuler, T. Scott Newlon, and William C. Randolph, "Do Repatriations Matter? Evidence from Tax Returns of Multinationals," in *The Effects of Taxation on Multinational Corporations*, Ed. by Martin Feldstein, James r. HInes, Jr. and R. Glenn Hubbard, Chicago: University of Chicago Press, 1995, pp. 253-277.

[33] Mehir A. Desai, C. Fritz Foley, and James R. Hines, Jr., "Repatriation Taxes and Dividend Distortions," *National Tax Journal*, Vol. 54, December 2001, pp. 829-851.

[34] Rosanne Altshuler and Harry Grubert, "Repatriation Taxes, Repatriation Strategies and Multinational Financial Policy, *Journal of Public Economics*, Vol 87, 2002, pp. 73-107.

[35] Some methods of returning cash to the United States involve corporate reorganizations. See Jesse Drucker, "Dodging Repatriation Tax Lets Companies Bring Home Cash," Bloomberg, December 29, 2010, http://www.bloomberg.com/news/2010-12-29/dodging-repatriation-tax-lets-u-s-companies-bring-home-cash.html. For an in depth discussion of methods, see Hal Hicks and David J. Sotos, "The Empire Strikes Back (Again) – The Killer Bs, Deadly Ds and Sec. 367 As The Death Star Against Repatriation Rebels,". *International Tax Journal*, May-June 2008, pp. 37-58. The Internal Revenue Service has periodically attempted to address various methods of repatriating cash without paying tax, most recently in July 2012. See Richard Rubin, "IRS Ends Deals That Let Companies Avoid Repatriation Tax," Bloomberg, July 13, 2011, at http://www.bloomberg.com/news/2012-07-13/irs-ends-deals-that-let-companies-avoid-repatriation-tax.html.

[36] Mehir A. Desai, C. Fritz Foley, and James R. Hines, Jr., Dividend Policy Inside the Multinational Firm, *Financial Management,* March 22, 2007, at http://www.thefreelibrary.com/Dividend+policy+inside+the+multinational+firm.-a0167305683.

[37] CRS Report R40178, *Tax Cuts on Repatriation Earnings as Economic Stimulus An Economic Analysis,* by Donald J. Marples and Jane G. Gravelle.

[38] The repatriations under the repatriation holiday, enacted on the basis of increasing investment, were largely used to (continued...)

---

reduce jobs. The economy will tend to create jobs naturally. As an illustration, consider that in 1961 and in 1991 the unemployment rate was the same, 6.7%. Employment, however, rose from 66 million to 117 million, as the economy accommodated the baby boom and the entry of women into the labor force. Permanent provisions that encourage capital to move abroad can change the types of jobs and reduce wages, but not overall employment.[39]

Location of Investment

Historically, the central issue in evaluating a foreign tax regime has been the effect on the allocation of investment. Economic theory seeking efficiency objectives supports taxing investments at the same rate wherever they are invested; this approach would maximize worldwide output by investing capital where it earns the highest pre-tax return. For example, if the after tax return is 7% and the U.S. tax is an effective 30% while the foreign tax rate is zero, and investments are perfect substitutes, the total pre-tax return at the margin on an investment in the United States is 10% (0.07/(1-0.30) while the return in the foreign location is only 7%. Allowing foreign source income to be exempt causes capital to move to a less productive use, where it earns a pre-tax return of 7%, when it could earn a 10% return in the United States.[40]

The equating of taxes on a firm's investment is most closely associated with a residence based tax system. Given the need for limits on foreign tax credits, this system would be most closely approximated by a system that eliminates deferral and imposes a foreign tax credit limit on a country by country basis. If the objective were not worldwide optimization or efficiency, but maximizing U.S. welfare, the rules would be more stringent by allowing foreign taxes as a deduction rather than a credit.[41]

Assessing Arguments for A Territorial Tax

What, then, is the justification for moving in the opposite direction, to a territorial tax? One may be that if, for political or other reasons, it is not possible to move closer to a residence-based system, it is possible to design a territorial tax system that is an improvement over the current rules. This argument is made by Grubert and Mutti,[42] and their proposal was incorporated in President Bush's Advisory Commission's tax reform proposals.[43] Grubert and Mutti proposed, along with exempting active dividends from tax, to provide for an allocation of overhead costs of

---

(...continued)

repurchase shares, the equivalent of paying dividends. See CRS Report R40178, *Tax Cuts on Repatriation Earnings as Economic Stimulus An Economic Analysis*, by Donald J. Marples and Jane G. Gravelle, for a review of the evidence.

[39] Using repatriations to increase employment in an underemployed economy in the short run are unlikely to be effective because transferring foreign earnings into U.S. dollars is contractionary and likely overwhelms any direct spending effects. See CRS Report R40178, *Tax Cuts on Repatriation Earnings as Economic Stimulus An Economic Analysis*, by Donald J. Marples and Jane G. Gravelle.

[40] Note that economic analysis has focused on efficient allocation of investment, rather than the effects on jobs because in the long run (the focus of a permanent tax law), an economy will tend to naturally create jobs.

[41] The issues discussed in this section are discussed in more detail in CRS Report RL34115, *Reform of U.S. International Taxation Alternatives*, by Jane G. Gravelle.

[42] Harry Grubert and John Mutti, Taxing *International Business Income Dividend Exemption Versus the Current System,*" Washington, DC, The AEI Press, 2001.

[43] The President's Advisory Panel on Federal Tax Reform, *Simple, Fair and Pro-Growth Proposals to Fix America's Tax System*, November, 2005, at http://govinfo.library.unt.edu/taxreformpanel/.

---

the firm (such as interest) between taxable and tax exempt income. For example, if 10% of income is exempt because of the dividend exemption then 10% of interest and other overhead costs would be disallowed. They also note that that the elimination of foreign tax credits would mean that royalty, export and other income would not be shielded from U.S. tax with excess foreign tax credits. As a result, this proposal is projected to raise revenue, a result also found by the Joint Committee on Taxation, and the overall tax rate on foreign source income would rise.[44] Grubert and Mutti also note that repatriations would not trigger a tax and that such a change would reduce the cost of tax planning to avoid the repatriation tax.

The argument that a territorial tax that could improve economic efficiency, or at least make it no worse, should be distinguished from arguments that do not stand up to economic reasoning. For example, moving to a territorial system because other countries have generally done so does not mean such a system is desirable either for them or for the United States. Many policies exist in other countries, such as a value added tax or national health insurance, policies that many oppose and that have not been adopted in the United States. The issues may differ as well. European countries, for example, are geographically and politically closer than the United States is to other countries. The European Union also has provisions on freedom of capital movement and establishment that prevent the type of anti-inversion laws that the United States has, to prevent U.S. firms from relocating their headquarters.[45] These rules may influence decisions to adopt territorial systems as well as decisions to lower corporate tax rates, which has occurred in the United Kingdom recently.

Similarly, the argument that because most other countries do not tax their foreign subsidiaries, the United States also should not do so in order to allow its firms to compete abroad does not stand up to economic analysis. A country does not compete in the manner that a firm does, because its resources (labor and savings provided by its citizens) do not disappear if another firm undercuts prices; they are simply used in a different way. That is, a country does not compete with the rest of the world, it trades with them, both its products and its capital. It can generally be shown that the United States would still be better off, or at least no worse off, if it taxes foreign and domestic investments by its firms at the same rate, even if other countries do not.[46]

Finally, arguments made based on empirical studies that indicate that increased foreign investment of multinationals is correlated with more, not less, domestic investment do not show that overall U.S investment is not reduced by more favorable foreign treatment, and may simply identify firms that are growing. In any event, the aggregate amount of capital owned by U.S. citizens and the allocation of that capital are separate issues. Even if savings responds to the overall U.S. tax burden, of two revenue neutral regimes, the one that taxes capital equally in both locations would be more efficient.

---

[44] The proposal is estimated to raise revenues by $6.9 billion in FY2014. See Congressional Budget Office, *Reducing the Deficit Spending and Revenue Options*, March, 2011, p. 187, http://www.cbo.gov/sites/default/files/cbofiles/ftpdocs/120xx/doc12085/03-10-reducingthedeficit.pdf.

[45] Countries can adopt anti-abuse provisions that are more limited. See Marco Rossi, "European Commission Blesses Italy's Anti-Inversion Rules," at http://www.euitalianinternationaltax.com/2011/05/articles/european-commission-blesses-italys-antiinversion-rules/.

[46] See Jane G. Gravelle, Does the Concept of Competitiveness Have Meaning in Formulating Corporate Tax Policy? November 2011, forthcoming, *Tax Law Review,* at http://www.americantaxpolicyinstitute.org/pdf/Jane%20Gravelle%20paper.pdf. Critiques of competitiveness arguments were also made, primarily with respect to trade policy, by Paul Krugman, See "Competitiveness: A Dangerous Obsession," *Foreign Affairs*, Vol. 73, No. 2 (March-April, 1994), pp. 28-44. Links to the journal can be found at http://www.foreignaffairs.com/issues/1994/73/4.

There are some arguments that have been made that bear consideration. Perhaps the most important of these is that U.S. firms can change their nationality by moving their headquarters abroad, merging with foreign companies, or incorporating abroad. However, anti-inversion rules adopted in 2004 are likely to prevent large-scale shifting of headquarters of existing firms, while mergers and incorporating abroad are probably largely determined by non-tax factors and could be addressed with legislative revisions.[47] Evidence suggests that very little incorporation of true U.S. firms occurs abroad[48] and this effect could be addressed with legislation (such as basing taxation on where effective management occurs) if necessary.

Arguments have also been made that the higher taxes on returns to capital investments would prevent U.S. firms from exploiting intangible assets abroad.[49] However, there are many ways of exploiting intangibles without engaging directly in manufacturing or other activities, such as licenses, franchises, and contract manufacturing.[50] Products embodying U.S. innovations could also be produced in the United States and exported.

Likely Effects of International Tax Revision on Investment

What are the likely effects of altering the international tax system on investment? There are several reasons that these effects would probably be modest, although they would depend on the particular design features of the reform.

First, most countries where physical investment might take place, such as manufacturing, tend to have taxes that are not much different from those that apply in the United States: average effective rates of 27% and marginal effective rates of about 20%.[51] The average effective tax rate on foreign subsidiaries of U.S. parents is estimated to be lower than that of U.S. firms in general (about 16% versus 26% with a 3% residual U.S. tax on foreign earnings), but that partially reflects profit shifting to low tax countries, since the effective rate in tax haven countries was 5.7%.[52] Overall effective tax rates abroad for foreign subsidiaries of U.S. companies also vary by

---

[47] Mergers that involve shifting the location of incorporation do occur occasionally. The announced merger of Eaton Corporation and Cooper Industries is an example of how mergers can be used to shift headquarters although even in this case the stated primary reason was non-tax issues. Cooper was already incorporated in Ireland, but is effectively a U.S. company with management in Houston. See Robert Schoenberger, "Eaton Corporation Plans to Buy Cooper Industries, Move Incorporation to Ireland," *The Plain Dealer*, May 12, 2012. http://www.cleveland.com/business/ index.ssf/2012/05/eaton_corp_plans_to_merge_with.html. Aon's shift of incorporation to the U.K. will trigger a shareholder level capital gains tax. See "Aon Shareholders May Pay Hefty Taxes With Headquarters Shifting to London," Ameet Sachdev's Chicago Law, at http://articles.chicagotribune.com/2012-01-20/business/ct-biz-0120-chicago-law-20120120_1_aon-global-aon-corp-tax. Among solutions to limit tax motivated international mergers is imposing a tax on shareholder gain at ordinary rates.

[48] Susan Morse and Eric Allen, "Firm Incorporation Outside the U.S.: No Exodus Yet," December 2011, at http://papers.ssrn.com/sol3/papers.cfm?abstract_id=1950760.

[49] This idea is most recently addressed in Mihir Desai and James Hines, "Evaluating International Tax Reform," *National Tax Journal*, Vol. 56, September 2003, pp. 487-502.

[50] See CRS Report RL34115, *Reform of U.S. International Taxation Alternatives*, by Jane G. Gravelle, for a more detailed discussion of this issue.

[51] See CRS Report R41743, *International Corporate Tax Rate Comparisons and Policy Implications*, by Jane G. Gravelle.

[52] Melissa Costa and Jennifer Gravelle, Taxing Multinational Corporations: Average Tax Rates, Presented at a Conference of the American Tax Policy Center, October 2011, and forthcoming in *Tax Law Review*, at http://www.americantaxpolicyinstitute.org/pdf/Costa-Gravelle%20paper.pdf.

---

industry. Industries with a lot of intangible assets have lower tax rates. For example, computer and electronic product manufacturing had an effective tax rate of 8.7% and finance 11.3%.[53]

Second, to the extent that firms expect largely to avoid U.S. taxes under the current system, either through permanent reinvestment of profits or tax planning, moving to a territorial tax would not make much difference in inducing outflows of capital, especially if anti-base erosion provisions (such as treating income earned in tax haven countries as Subpart F Income) are adopted. Nevertheless, since firms' investments are only observed under the current deferral and foreign tax credit system, it is possible that significantly more capital would be invested abroad, especially in lower tax jurisdictions.

Moving in the opposite direction, by ending deferral and possibly cross-crediting (with a per country foreign tax credit limit) would reduce capital investment abroad by retaining more outbound capital in the United States.

Nevertheless, effects from either revision are unlikely to be important to the overall U.S. economy or to U.S. welfare; estimates of the effect of cutting the U.S. corporate tax rate by ten percentage points, which would presumably have larger effects by attracting inbound capital as well is estimated to increase U.S. output by only about 2/10ths of 1% and U.S. income by 2/100ths of 1%.[54] The effects of moving to a territorial tax would be negative (decrease U.S. output) because they increase the return on outbound capital, but would be smaller in magnitude because the effects are smaller. Based on relative sizes of revenue effects, a ten percentage point rate reduction would lose about 29% of corporate revenue, while, based on the estimates in **Table 5**, eliminating all taxes on foreign source income would lose about 7.5% of corporate revenue, or a quarter of the amount. Eliminating deferral alone would gain revenue equal to about 15% of the absolute change from a ten percentage point rate reduction, while eliminating deferral and cross-crediting would be about 53% of the change. This last change could be more significant than the domestic rate reduction but nevertheless not large relative to the U.S. economy.

All of these effects are small, relative to output, for several reasons. First, although capital flows respond to differential tax rates, capital is not perfectly mobile.[55] Even if it were, the large size of the U.S. domestic economy and capital stock and the constraints of production (capital must combine with labor to be productive) limit the effect to ½ of 1% of output and a negligible effect

---

[53] Charles Duhigg and David Kocieniewski, "How Apples Sidesteps Billions in Taxes," *New York Times*, April 29, 2012, p.1, 20-21. at http://www.nytimes.com/2012/04/29/business/apples-tax-strategy-aims-at-low-tax-states-and-nations.html?pagewanted=all.

[54] See CRS Report R41743, *International Corporate Tax Rate Comparisons and Policy Implications*, by Jane G. Gravelle.

[55] The overall evidence suggests an elasticity of around three which is used in the calculations above; see Jennifer C. Gravelle, Corporate Tax Incidence: Review of General Equilibrium Estimates and Analysis, Working Paper 2010-03, May 2010, at http://www.cbo.gov/sites/default/files/cbofiles/ftpdocs/115xx/doc11519/05-2010-working_paper-corp_tax_incidence-review_of_gen_eq_estimates.pdf. See Harry Grubert and Rosanne Altshuler, "Corporate Taxes in the World Economy: Reforming the Taxation of Cross-border Income," in *Fundamental Tax Reform Issues, Choices, and Implications*, Ed. John W. Diamond and George R. Zodrow, Cambridge, MIT Press, 2008 who reference a number of studies showing that investment by multinationals is sensitive to tax rates. A review is also contained in Michael Smart, Repatriation Taxes and Foreign Direct Investment: Evidence From Tax Treaties, Working Paper, June 20, 2010, at http://www.sbs.ox.ac.uk/centres/tax/symposia/Documents/2010/05%20Smart.pdf; and in Lars Feld and Jost Heckemeyer, "FDI and Taxation: A Meta Study," *Journal of Economic Surveys*, Vol 25, April, 2011, pp.233-272 . The working paper version is at http://www.cesifo-group.de/portal/pls/portal/docs/1/1186528.PDF.

on income.[56] The corporate tax itself is also small as a cost factor: about 2% of GDP. Thus even a 10 percentage point rate reduction would be slightly over ½ of 1% of GDP, while most international revisions would be even smaller. Finally, most of these gains would not accrue to U.S. income: for inbound capital most of the gain would be profit to foreign investors, and for outbound capital drawn back, profits were already in existence and merely change location.

The analysis in this section suggests that while there may be concerns about the effects of international reforms on investments, either reducing U.S. investment in the case of a territorial tax or increasing it by moving towards a residence based tax (e.g., eliminating deferral and cross-crediting) these effects are likely quite modest.

Treatment of Royalties and Export Income

One effect of the current system that might be changed by moving to a territorial system is the reduction in the beneficial treatment of royalties and export income through the use of excess foreign tax credits. The current benefits for royalties encourage firms to exploit intangibles in foreign operations rather than in the United States, while the export subsidy causes prices and magnitudes of exports to be too large.

Royalties, in particular, are a difficult issue to address because increased taxes on royalties paid from foreign subsidiaries would encourage manufacturing of goods in the United States but, as will be discussed in the next section, also creates an incentive to understate royalties and artificially shift intangible income into untaxed active earnings of foreign subsidiaries that are exempt. Ideally, such profit shifting should be addressed by anti-abuse provisions.

Artificial Profit Shifting

The third issue, which primarily involves revenue, is artificial profit shifting—that is, shifting profits into low-tax jurisdictions that are then exempt from U.S. tax. Profit shifting also exists under the current system because of deferral. Evidence of profit shifting is clear from the distribution of shares of U.S. subsidiary profits as a percentage of GDP, where profits as a percentage of output were typically less than 1%-2% in the G-7, were significantly larger in the larger tax-haven countries (7.6% in Ireland and 18.2% in Luxemburg), and were more than 600% and 500% respectively in Bermuda and the Cayman Islands.[57] The estimates of magnitude vary substantially reaching up to $90 billion and ranging from about 14% to 29% of corporate revenues.[58] They have been growing as well.[59]

---

[56] Estimates from CRS Report R41743, *International Corporate Tax Rate Comparisons and Policy Implications*, by Jane G. Gravelle, based on perfect mobility of capital and perfect product substitution.

[57] CRS Report R40623, *Tax Havens International Tax Avoidance and Evasion* and CRS Report R41743, *International Corporate Tax Rate Comparisons and Policy Implications*, both by Jane G. Gravelle. Data on earnings and profits of controlled foreign corporations were taken from Lee Mahoney and Randy Miller, Controlled Foreign Corporations 2004, Internal Revenue Service Statistics of Income Bulletin, Summer 2008,http://www.irs.ustreas.gov/pub/irs-soi/04coconfor.pdf. Data on GDP from Central Intelligence Agency, The World Factbook, https://www.cia.gov/library/publications/the-world-factbook. Most GDP data are for 2008 and based on the exchange rate but for some countries earlier years and data based on purchasing power parity were the only data available.

[58] See CRS Report R40623, *Tax Havens International Tax Avoidance and Evasion* and CRS Report R41743, *International Corporate Tax Rate Comparisons and Policy Implications*, both by Jane G. Gravelle. For the most recent estimates see Kimberly A. Clausing "The Revenue Effects of Multinational Firm Income Shifting *Tax Notes*, March (continued...)

In general, most of this profit shifting apparently arises from either leveraging (borrowing in high-tax jurisdictions) or shifting of the location of profits from intangibles. It is not surprising, therefore, that low-tax rates tend to be associated with manufacture of drugs and electronics, and the information and communications industries.

Profit shifting is a policy problem even without a move to a territorial tax. One of the concerns about moving to a territorial tax is the possibility that it will increase the already significant and growing estimated level of profit shifting. Under current law, firms that have shifted profits to low-tax jurisdictions may still have to face eventual taxation. The considerable lobbying for a repatriation holiday such as that in 2004 may be a sign of this concern.[60] With a simple territorial tax with no anti-abuse provisions, profit shifting could increase substantially. There is little to clarify the likely magnitude of this effect. Evidence for European countries has also indicated significant profit shifting, benefiting most European countries largely at the expense of Germany.[61] Germany has since lowered their corporate tax rate (and profit shifting may have played a role in that decision). However, it is difficult to draw conclusions from the experiences of these very different countries, who already have territorial systems but also have in most cases had measures to address base erosion.

If the new view of dividends is correct, and companies expect to pay taxes on excess profits with interest when deferred, then the move to a simple territorial tax (without any anti-base erosion measures) could increase profit shifting, perhaps considerably. However, if this view is not correct and firms expect to escape tax indefinitely, then going to a territorial tax might not make much difference. Unfortunately, while there is a relatively powerful theoretical justification for the new view, the empirical evidence has been mixed. At the same time, however, as noted above, the lobbying for a repatriation holiday supports the new view and the expectation that profit shifting might increase insignificantly.

One particular potential effect on profit shifting involves royalties. Because royalties are protected to some extent by excess foreign tax credits, moving to a territorial tax would eliminate that protection and increase the tax on royalties. This change in taxation would create a further incentive to shift intangible income into the earnings of foreign subsidiaries and out of royalties.

Aside from the issue of the effect of a territorial tax (and of its particular design features) on profit shifting, other reforms might be considered that might address profit shifting either in the current system or in a system revised in ways other than moving to a territorial tax. These reforms might include provisions reforming the current system proposed by President Obama (and earlier by former Ways and Means Committee Chairman Rangel), which would tax excess earnings from

---

(...continued)

28, 2011, pp. 1580-1586, who finds estimates for 2008 from $57 billion to $90 billion and Martin Sullivan, "Transfer Pricing Costs U.S. at Least $28 Billion," *Tax Notes*, March 22, 2010, pp. 1439-1443.

[59] Martin Sullivan, "Transfer Pricing Abuse Is Job-Killing Corporate Welfare," *Tax Notes* August 2, 2010, pp. 461-468.

[60] The lobbying group has apparently ended at least part of their campaign. See "WIN America, Tax Repatriation Holiday Lobby Group, Ends Advocacy Work" Reuters, http://www.huffingtonpost.com/2012/04/23/win-america-tax-repatriation-holiday_n_1447581.html?ref=business. For a report on the repatriation holiday and its issues see CRS Report R40178, *Tax Cuts on Repatriation Earnings as Economic Stimulus An Economic Analysis*, by Donald J. Marples and Jane G. Gravelle.

[61] Harry Huizinga and Luc Laeven, "International Profit Shifting Within Multinationals: A Multi-Country Perspective," *Journal of Public Economics*, vol. 92. 2008, pp.1164-1182.

---

intangibles as subpart F income and rules that would disallow some portion of overhead expenses to the extent income is not taxed.

Fundamentally, as long as a system allows for differential taxes, whether between the U.S. and foreign source income or between types of foreign source income, there is likely to be profit shifting. Companies appear willing to exploit relatively small differentials in tax as illustrated by the double-Irish, Dutch sandwich technique that allowed firms to not only avoid the U.S. tax, but to avoid the 12.5% Irish tax as well, and establish taxation in Bermuda, with a zero tax rate.[62] The only tax system that eliminates differential taxes is the elimination of deferral, possibly combined with a separate tax credit limit basket for royalty income.

Transition

An important issue in moving to a territorial tax is how to treat accumulated unrepatriated earnings, which were generated under a worldwide system. One approach would be to deem all accumulated earnings as repatriated and pay taxes, with a number of years allowed to pay these taxes. The provision might create a hardship for firms to the extent that income is tied up in non-liquid form, unless the period of time for paying the tax were extensive. In addition, it would be a retroactively harsh tax compared with the present system, because a significant portion of earnings need never be repatriated. During normal times, estimates suggest that more than half of retained earnings abroad is probably reinvested in the firms activities. Note also that while perhaps 60% or so of the flow of income would be retained abroad, a much larger share of the stock of unrepatriated earnings would be likely to be permanently reinvested abroad.

Another option is to treat these earnings the same as newly generated earnings and exempt them in the same way. This approach would create a windfall benefit, especially to the degree that firms have been holding off repatriating and engaging in aggressive profit shifting because of a potential tax holiday.

A third option would be to treat dividends as paid out of accumulated earnings until these earnings are exhausted, while applying the full tax rate and foreign tax credit rules. This approach, however, would continue the disincentive to repatriate for some time.

None of these approaches may be entirely satisfactory. Intermediate proposals that are under consideration would tax this income but at a lower rate. One, in the Ways and Means proposal, is to deem all this earnings repatriated prior to the law changes, apply the provisions of the 2004 tax holiday (85% exclusion of income with proportional foreign tax credits), which would impose a small tax, and allow it to be paid over a period of time. On average this may be a reasonable compromise, because, although a significant fraction of income is exempt, a significant fraction of this income would probably never have been repatriated.

A second intermediate option is to allow firms to elect the holiday (with an extended pay out period) and to tax any remaining dividends at the full tax rate until all of the remaining earnings is paid out as dividends. This voluntary approach allows firms to avoid undesirable forced payouts, but prolongs the effective movement to a territorial tax.

---

[62] Jesse Drucker, "Google 2.4% Rate Shows How $60 Billion Lost to Tax Loopholes," *Bloomberg*, October 21, 2010, at http://www.bloomberg.com/news/2010-10-21/google-2-4-rate-shows-how-60-billion-u-s-revenue-lost-to-tax-loopholes.html.

Striking a balance between limiting the windfall benefits and the associated revenue loss compared with a baseline, providing firms with terms that allow the funds to pay (since a lot of accumulated earnings are not liquid) and avoiding prolonged coverage of dividends under the old system is one of the most difficult problems in crafting a shift to a territorial tax. As will be discussed subsequently, the proposals have included a variety of approaches.

While accumulated untaxed earnings are an important issue, there are other transition issues relating to the shift from the current system to a territorial tax. These include unused foreign tax credits associated with previously taxed income and foreign loss carryovers. How credits and losses might be treated may depend largely on the treatment of existing earnings accumulated abroad and how other features of the foreign tax credit are modified.

Administration and Compliance

Arguments have often been made that moving to a territorial tax would simplify administration and compliance. Grubert and Mutti, in their proposal for a territorial tax, stressed the cost of tax planning associated with repatriating income while paying minimal tax. Thus a territorial tax would add value by simplifying repatriation policy. U.S. parents could receive dividends from their subsidiaries without concerns about the tax consequences. However, the same simplification would occur if deferral were ended, because firms would have no choice about paying taxes or arranging for optimal cross-crediting. Hybrid approaches such as taxing a share of income currently would also eliminate the scope for tax planning around repatriation.

Although repatriation tax planning would be eliminated, if a territorial tax increased profit shifting incentives, tax planning in that could increase. And, as will be shown in the discussion of design issues, provisions considered to combat income shifting can add considerable complexity to the tax code.

Revenue Issues

A shift to a territorial system could potentially gain revenue, in part because relatively little tax is collected on foreign operations. In any case, it is unlikely that large revenue losses would occur unless the move to a territorial tax includes other provisions (such as lower tax rates on royalties) or induces pronounced income shifting responses. If **Table 4** shares of income are applied to estimates of current taxes paid on foreign source income listed in **Table 5**, the taxation of dividends of foreign subsidiaries is quite small, a little over $4 billion in FY2014, or about 1% of corporate revenues. Branch income is slightly under $6 billion, so if this income is also exempted in a move to a territorial tax, the total effect would be about $10 billion. The two together are about 2% of corporate revenues. Taxes on royalties and export income (which along with nonfinancial interest would be somewhat over $10 billion, or about 2% of revenues) could increase with the loss of foreign tax credits, leading to a relatively small net loss or possibly a small gain.

There is considerably more revenue to be gained by moving in the opposite direction, as some proposals do. Eliminating deferral and providing a per country foreign tax credit limit could triple the revenue collected on foreign source income, raising $64 billion or about 15% of corporate taxes, according to the estimates in **Table 5**. Other intermediate changes could raise revenues;

eliminating deferral alone would raise about $18 billion in revenue, and the combination of President Obama's budget proposals for international taxation would raise $16 billion.[63]

Some proposals for moving to a territorial tax aim for revenue neutrality, but also propose to use transitional revenues (from taxes on accumulated untaxed earnings) to achieve this revenue neutrality in the budget horizon. Because transitional gains are temporary, this approach results in a long-run revenue loss.

Design Issues in a Territorial Tax

Moving to a territorial tax goes far beyond a simple matter of exempting foreign source income from U.S. tax. There are issues of transition, the treatment of current flow through income, and the retention and perhaps revision of anti-abuse rules. In this section, three proposals are outlined: the Grubert Mutti proposal, the discussion draft provided by Ways and Means Committee Chairman, and Senator Enzi's bill, S. 2091. The latter two proposals are similar in general approach. Note that the Grubert Mutti proposal is a general outline, while the Ways and Means Discussion Draft and S. 2091 are in legislative language and are more detailed.

The Grubert Mutti Proposal

This proposal has been circulating for some time as a general proto-type of a move to a territorial tax, and has been estimated to raise revenue, primarily due to increased taxes on royalties and allocation of parent company expenses between taxable and exempt income.[64] A proposal of this nature was included in President Bush's Advisory Panel Proposal in 2005.[65]

- Exemption of dividends for active foreign income by U.S. shareholders with a 10% or more interest and eliminate foreign tax credits.

- Foreign branches treated the same as subsidiaries.

- Royalties and interest paid to the U.S. parent are taxable.

- Current anti-abuse rules for passive income(Subpart F) would be retained, although some aspects would become obsolete (primarily the inclusion of dividend payments between subsidiaries).

- Parent's overhead expenses, such as interest, would be allocated in proportion to untaxed income and disallowed.

- Active foreign losses could not offset domestic income.

- Capital gains and losses from the sale of productive assets would be exempt.

- Income from U.S. exports would not be classified as foreign source income.

---

[63] Department of the Treasury, *General Explanations of the Administration's Fiscal Year 2013 Revenue Proposals*, February 2012, http://www.treasury.gov/resource-center/tax-policy/Documents/General-Explanations-FY2013.pdf.

[64] Harry Grubert and John Mutti, Taxing *International Business Income Dividend Exemption Versus the Current System* (Washington, DC, AEI Press, 2001).

[65] The President's Advisory Panel on Federal Tax Reform, *Simple, Fair and Pro-Growth Proposals to Fix America's Tax System*, November, 2005, at http://govinfo.library.unt.edu/taxreformpanel/.

The proposal does not address the treatment of existing accumulated earnings abroad or profit shifting via intangible assets, although one of the proposal's authors has indicated that their plan should probably include a tax on accumulated earnings, but at a lower rate.[66]

This proposal has been estimated to raise revenue of approximately $6.9 billion in 2014.[67] If the shares of revenue in **Table 4** remain the same for 2014, about 30% of current tax on foreign source income or slightly under $10 billion (based on aggregates from **Table 5**) is collected on active dividends and branch income. The additional taxes on royalties and export income plus limits on the deduction of overhead expenses presumably raise about $17 billion (replacing the lost revenue and generating additional amounts).

Ways and Means Chairman Camp's Discussion Draft

In October 2011, Ways and Means Chairman Dave Camp released a discussion draft outlining an approach to a territorial tax (hereafter Discussion Draft). This proposal includes some options and unsettled issues, and there is not as yet a revenue estimate. Note also that the intention expressed in press releases at that time was to couple the move to a territorial tax with a general tax reform that would reduce the top corporate rate from 35% to 25%. This rate matters since some provisions allow a proportional tax benefit. Since the other changes that might be needed to achieve this reduction have not been yet spelled out, no observations on the effects if any remaining revision will be included, outside of noting the consequences of the rate change for specific territorial provisions.

The following summary of these provisions does not include all of the detailed nuances of the proposal, which are contained in a technical draft discussion.[68]

- Allows a 95% deduction for the foreign source portion of dividends for 10% U.S. corporate shareholders of foreign subsidiaries that are controlled foreign corporations (CFCs). A holding period of one year for stock in foreign corporations is required. If the rate is reduced to 25%, dividends would be taxed at 1.25%; at the current rate, they would be taxed at 1.75%. (CFCs are those where 50% of the stock is owned by five or fewer 10% U.S. shareholders.)

- 10% corporate shareholders of non controlled corporations (where 50% of the stock is not owned by five or fewer 10% U.S. shareholders, called 10/50 corporations) can elect the same treatment as CFCs.

- Foreign branches are treated the same as subsidiaries; the draft also considers the possible inclusion of partnerships in this treatment.

- Anti-abuse (Subpart F) provisions are retained, although these rules would be revised in light of the other changes; these details are to be considered subsequently. Dividends paid between CFCs are exempt.

---

[66] Author's conversation with Harry Grubert, July 2, 2012.

[67] Congressional Budget Office, *Reducing the Deficit Spending and Revenue Options*, March 20, 2011, p. 187. http://www.cbo.gov/sites/default/files/cbofiles/ftpdocs/120xx/doc12085/03-10-reducingthedeficit.pdf

[68] Documents, including bill language, technical discussions and shorter summaries can be found at the Ways and Means Committee website at http://waysandmeans.house.gov/taxreform/.

- Capital gains on sales of stock in active eligible subsidiaries are also eligible for a 95% exclusion.

- Accumulated untaxed earnings will be taxed with an 85% exclusion and apportionment of associated foreign tax credits in the same fashion as the 2004 repatriation holiday, except that all earnings will be taxed rather than earnings that are voluntarily repatriated. No actual repatriation is necessary. Firms can pay the tax in installments with interest over eight years. Assuming this provision applies before changes in the statutory tax rate, the effective rate is 5.25% less any apportioned foreign tax credits.

- The foreign tax credits associated with active dividends and with foreign branch income are disallowed (those for Subpart F are retained). All foreign tax credits would be in one basket, presumably because the active basket would no longer be relevant. The proposal also eliminates the allocation of parent interest that presently applies to determine the foreign tax credit limit: only directly associated expenses will be applied to determine foreign income. It would also repeal the provision preventing the splitting of foreign tax credits.

- A provision that requires the inclusion in income of investments of deferred income (income that is not taxed because it is not distributed) in U.S. property is repealed. This provision exists to prevent firms from effectively repatriating earnings without declaring dividends that are subject to the tax.

- Three anti-base-erosion options, two directed at intangible income, are considered. Option A is similar to a proposal made by President Obama in his budget proposals, that would tax excess earnings on intangibles (in excess of 150% of costs) in low tax jurisdictions as Subpart F. The inclusion would be phased out between a 10% and a 15% rate. Option B would tax income that is subject to an effective foreign tax rate below 10% unless it qualifies for a home country exception. The home country exception applies when a firm conducts an active trade or business in the home country, has a fixed place of business, and serves the local market. Option C would tax all foreign income from intangibles (whether earnings by the foreign subsidiary or royalty payments) but allow a deduction for 40%, resulting in a tax rate of 15% at a 25% statutory tax rate.

- Additional base-erosion provisions (sometimes call thin-capitalization rules) relating to interest would restrict the deduction for interest if the company failed to meet either of two tests: if debt to equity ratios in the U.S. differed from the total debt to equity ratio worldwide and if interest expenses exceed a certain share of adjusted income (generally taxable income before the deduction of interest and depreciation). The smaller of the excess interest under either test would be disallowed, but the percentage has not been specified.

- The draft indicates that the two extenders, exception from Subpart F of active financing and active insurance income and the look-through rules, would be considered separately.

Senator Enzi's Bill (S. 2091)

Senator Enzi has introduced S. 2091 which is similar in many respects to the Ways and Means Discussion Draft. His bill is a separate bill that does not include a general tax reform or lowering of the corporate rate.[69]

- The Enzi proposal provides the same 95% dividend exemption and election option for 10/50 companies as the Discussion Draft.

- Foreign branches would not be treated as subsidiaries.

- Anti-abuse rules (Subpart F) would be retained, but the inclusion of foreign base company sales and service income would be eliminated.

- Capital gains on the sale of stock would be eligible for the exclusion to the extent they would be treated as a dividend under Section 1248 (which treats gains as dividends to the extent of earnings and profits).

- Firms could elect to tax accumulated earnings with a 70% exclusion (a 10.5% tax) and no foreign tax credits; otherwise accumulated earnings would be taxed at full rates with foreign tax credits allowed when paid out as dividends and these pre-existing earnings would be deemed to be paid out first.

- Foreign tax credits (and deductions for these taxes) associated with exempt income would be disallowed.

- The Enzi bill does not repeal the provision taxing investments of deferred income in U.S. property.

- For anti-base-erosion provisions a version of Option B in the Discussion Draft along with a version of the first part of Option C would be included. Income in countries with tax rates of half or less than the U.S. rate (17.5%) would be subject to tax. However, operations that conduct an active business, with employees and officers that contribute substantially, would be excepted except to the extent the income is intangible income of the CFC. The CFC's intangible income would be Subpart F income. These rules provide more scope for exemption as compared to the rules in the Discussion Draft which would require exempt income to carry out activities serving the home country market. The bill also includes the first part of Option C, allowing a 17.5% tax rate on intangible income (such as royalties) earned by a domestic corporation. Intangible income would be placed in a separate foreign tax credit basket.

- The bill does not contain the thin capitalization rules (such as allocating interest between U.S. firms and their foreign subsidiaries).

- The bill makes the two extenders, the exception from Subpart F for active financing and active insurance income and the look-through rules, permanent. It also applies the worldwide interest allocation for purposes of the foreign tax credit in 2013, rather than 2021.

---

[69] Ernst & Young has provided a summary of this bill, "Senator Enzi Introduces and International Tax Reform Bill," http://www.ey.com/Publication/vwLUAssets/Senator_Enzi_introduces_an_international_tax_reform_bill/ $FILE/Senator%20Enzi%20introduces%20reform%20bill.pdf, March 1, 2012.

Analysis and Commentary on the Proposals

Some insights into issues and trade offs may be noted by observing the difference between these proposals. In addition, the Discussion Draft proposals invited commentary, which has appeared in a number of venues including testimony before a Ways and Means Subcommittee on Select Revenue Measures hearing on November 27, 2011. This section examines the alternative approaches in light of the issues discussed earlier and general design considerations.

Repatriation Incentives

While the Grubert-Mutti proposal has no tax that is triggered by repatriation, the other two territorial proposals do, due to the 5% "haircut" resulting from the proposed 95% exemption. In addition, the Discussion Draft also allows firms to choose an alternate completely tax free method of repatriation since investment in U.S. assets is not taxed, even at a 5% share. Presumably, the expectation is that the tax due to the 5% inclusion in income (1.25% at a 25% rate and 1.75% tax at a 35% rate) is too small to matter. At least one commentator, however, has singled this issue out as a potentially serious one indicating that as long as tax planning to avoid even a small tax is costless, firms will undertake it.[70] One option for the Discussion Draft, which would not eliminate the small repatriation tax but would eliminate the costless avoidance, would be to continue to tax these transactions, or to tax 5% of them. An approach that could eliminate the repatriation tax trigger arising from the 5% exclusion altogether is to include 5% of income whether repatriated or not, and make dividends entirely exempt.

S. 2091 also has an additional temporary repatriation trigger arising from its transition rule, which allows firms to elect to repatriate under a 70% exclusion without credits, but would tax dividends until any remaining accumulated funds are exhausted. Presumably, firms would repatriate funds voluntarily from low tax jurisdictions, and then repatriate funds from countries with high foreign taxes until the backlog is exhausted.

The Grubert Mutti proposal does not have any special provision for accumulated untaxed earnings and dividends paid out of those earnings . Basically this provision was not addressed although, as noted above, the authors would expect some transition rule similar to the other proposals; this treatment was not incorporated into their revenue estimates.

Effects on Tax Burden and Investment

Although the Discussion Draft leaves a number of options open, its objective to be revenue neutral indicates that it is more beneficial to U.S. multinational firms than the Grubert-Mutti proposal that raises revenue. Moreover the Discussion Draft proposes to finance part of the revenue loss through the one time revenue gain from the tax on existing accumulated earnings. Senator Enzi has indicated an intention for his bill to be revenue neutral as well, although it has not been scored.[71]

---

[70] Jeffery M. Kadet, "Territorial W&M Discussion Draft: Change Required," *Tax Notes*, January 23, 2012, pp. 463-464.

[71] See Senator Enzi's press release, at http://www.enzi.senate.gov/uploads/3.pdf.

Some elements that increase the tax burden on foreign source income (offsetting the loss from exempting dividends and in some cases branch income) are the allocation of deductions and taxation of royalties in the Grubert-Mutti proposal and the 5% inclusion of dividends in the other two proposals. The base erosion provisions may or may not increase taxes depending on which option is chosen and the extent to which firms can use the active trade or business exception to avoid the tax. Some of the reason for these differences in revenue effect is that the 5% inclusion appears to be significantly smaller than overhead costs (even excluding interest). One comment also noted that the 5% inclusion does not take account of a firm's individual circumstances.[72]

Altshuler and Grubert estimate that overhead expenses outside of interest and research expenditures are 10% of pretax earnings.[73] Moreover, their proposal would disallow the deduction regardless of whether dividends are paid out, while the 5% inclusion would apply only to dividends paid. Assuming that about 40% of earnings are paid out in a steady state the 5% provision would be 2% of total earnings. Thus the provision in the Grubert-Mutti proposal would be about five times the size of the provision in the Discussion Draft and S. 2091.

Presumably interest would also be significant. The Grubert-Mutti proposal has a direct allocation rule for the parent's interest presumably based on allocations of assets.[74] The proposal does not spell out specifics, but interest allocation could be net or gross, and it could involve only the parent interest or worldwide interest. Turning to years of 2006 and 2007, net interest as a share of combined interest and pretax earnings of nonfinancial corporations in the National Income and Product Accounts was 15% in 2006 and 21% in 2007.[75] The 2006 measure may be more appropriate as a steady state guide since profits had begun to decline in 2007. According to tax statistics, for manufacturing the share was 13% in 2006 and 18% in 2007.[76] Gross interest, the basis of the current allocation rules for the foreign tax credit limit, would be much larger, ranging from 34% to 39% of profits plus interest payments. In a related article, by Altshuler and Grubert, the analysis assumes that debt accounts for a third of the capital stock.[77] The Discussion Draft has thin capitalization rules that are based on two alternative tests: an allocation provision for net interest based on parent versus subsidiary debt-equity ratios taking into account worldwide debt and an alternative based on an as-yet-unspecified share of adjusted income, so that the effects on interest are uncertain. S. 2091 has no allocation rule.

Grubert and Mutti could have an allocation for research and development expenditures but apparently do not.[78] Thus, they have no provision that addresses profit shifting from intangibles.

---

[72] Comments of Stephen Shay, KPMG, Will the U.S. Shift to a Territorial System: A Discussion of Chairman Camp's Territorial Tax Draft, http://www.us.kpmg.com/microsite/taxnewsflash/Corporate/2011/tgi-exec-sum-territorial-tax.pdf.

[73] Rosanne Altshuler and Harry Grubert, "Where Will They Go if We Go Territorial? Dividend Exemption and the Location Decisions of U.S. Multinational Corporations," *National Tax Journal*, December 2001, pp. 787-809.

[74] The proposal refers to allocating the parents interest to firms and not worldwide interest, although a worldwide allocation would be an option.

[75] See data from Economic Report of the President at http://www.gpo.gov/fdsys/pkg/ERP-2012/pdf/ERP-2012-table15.pdf.

[76] Internal Revenue Service, http://www.irs.gov/taxstats/article/0,,id=170692,00.html. In 2006, the manufacturing sector has 247 billion of interest payments, $183 billion of interest income and $481 billion in net income. In 2007, these numbers were $304 billion, $203 billion and $468 billion respectively.

[77] Rosanne Altshuler and Harry Grubert, "Where Will They Go if We Go Territorial? Dividend Exemption and the Location Decisions of U.S. Multinational Corporations," *National Tax Journal*, December 2001, pp. 787-809.

[78] Ibid.

If these costs were included, for 2006 for manufacturing they were 18% of the total of earnings and research costs.[79] Neither the discussion draft nor S. 2091 have such an allocation, although they have some options that affect base erosion that could address intangibles.

Without more specific guidelines, it is difficult to determine the share of income that would be taxed under the Grubert Mutti proposal. Using net interest, the ratio for manufacturing in 2006 relative to net income is about 15% and the overhead costs add another 10%, taxing about 25% of income, whether paid as a dividend or not. In contrast, assuming 40% of income is paid as a dividend, the 5% inclusion in the Discussion Draft and S. 2091 would tax about 2%. At a 35% rate, these effects would impose additional taxes of 8.75% (0.25 times 0.35) under the Grubert Mutti plan and 0.7% (0.05 times 0.35 times 0.40).

If the allocation of interest is made based on worldwide costs (and not just U.S. parent costs), the allocation could be smaller and firms could shift interest costs to their foreign subsidiaries and deduct them so that the effect would be only the difference between the U.S. and foreign rate. In addition, with an overall allocation, this interest cost would presumably be shifted to high tax countries. The United States would still gain revenue but some of it would be offset (from the firm's point of view) by lower tax payments to foreign countries. At the extreme, only the overhead allocation of 10% would affect taxes, leading to a 3.5 percentage point tax increase.

Both the Discussion Draft and S. 2091 include specific anti-base erosion measures which are not included in the Grubert Mutti proposal and these may to some extent substitute for cost allocation provisions. These provisions relate less to investment than to profit shifting and are discussed in the next section.

Incentives could also be affected by the treatment of royalties whose tax burden would rise as excess foreign tax credits disappear. This higher tax on royalties could encourage both more exports of products with technology embodied (as the cost of exploiting intangibles abroad increases). It could also encourage more research to be performed abroad in low tax CFCs although this effect is unclear since such research would not have a benefit as an investment (expensing and the R&D credit) as is the case in the United States.

S. 2091 also provides that royalty income will be taxed at a 17.5% rate, which reduces the additional taxes that would arise from the loss of foreign tax credits on other incomes. A lower tax on royalties is an option in the discussion draft. Under S. 2091, intangibles that fall under the anti-base erosion rules would be taxed at the full rate, 35%.

As noted earlier, none of the shifts in investment are likely to be large relative to the U.S. economy. Thus, even if the provisions induce more research to be performed abroad, the consequences would not be likely to be significant.

Artificial Profit Shifting

There are several different anti-profit shifting regimes discussed in the proposals: the full allocation of deductions in Mutti and Grubert, the interest allocation rules plus one of three options in the Ways and Means Draft, and the combination of components of two of the three

---

[79] International Revenue Service statistics, at http://www.irs.gov/taxstats/article/0,,id=164402,00.html.

options for S. 2091. Although a more detailed discussion is presented below, **Table 6** summarizes the discussion.

Grubert and Mutti address artificial profit shifting by allocating deductions, including overhead administrative costs and interest. For interest deductions, this allocation method should address the shifting facilitated through leveraging, although their proposal may only allocate parent company expenses. A more comprehensive approach is to allocate world wide expenses.[80] They discuss this world wide approach as well, which would lose revenue compared to allocating only parent company costs and could potentially cause an overall revenue loss. For intangible profits, they do not address the tax on income shifted abroad. Rather they disallow a portion of the associated investment costs (research and development costs and other overhead costs such as marketing). Their anti-abuse program has the virtue of simplicity and because an increase in profits abroad triggers a tax (in the form of foregone deductions) it reduces the incentive to shift profits through that effect as well.

Table 6. Summary of Discussion in Text of Base Erosion Provisions of the Proposals

Grubert and Mutti

Allocation of Deductions	Allocation of overhead costs and interest is simple. It might be desirable to employ worldwide allocation. Allocation would automatically impose an additional tax on shifted profits. Grubert and Mutti have no provisions to address profit shifting through intangibles.

Ways and Means Discussion Draft

Interest restrictions	Worldwide allocation of interest may be effective in dealing with leverage. The abi ity to meet an alternative less restrictive test may undermine the effects; it is not clear what the purpose of this alternative is.
Plus Option A	Provisions to tax as U.S. connected income intangible earnings in excess of 150% of costs for countries with rates below 15% (phased out between 10% and 15%) would discourage profit shifting of this nature. It creates an incentive to shift costs to low tax countries and could encourage firms to relocate. Measuring effective tax rates and identifying affected income would be complicated.
Or Plus Option B	Provisions to tax income in countries with rates below 10% as U.S. income would exclude Ireland, and would encourage firms to shift to s ightly higher tax rate countries, or perhaps encourage tax havens to increase taxes, both of which would increase taxes paid to foreigners. Measuring effective tax rates could be complicated. Firms may be able to avoid the U.S. tax through the home country exception.
Or Plus Option C	This provision, which taxes all intangible income as U.S. income at a lower rate is not triggered by the country's tax rate and effectively imposes a minimum tax of 15% on intangible income. It thus imposes a lower tax rate on income in low tax jurisdictions but does not induce shifting to other countries. It also imposes the same tax rate on royalties, reducing the incentive to shift these profits into a subsidiary, but compared to a plan without this feature, encouraging production abroad. Distinguishing intangible income would be difficult. This royalty provision might violate WTO rules against export subsidies.

S. 2091 (Enzi)

No Deduction Allocation	This bill has no provision for restricting leveraging directly.

---

[80] When the Grubert Mutti proposal was developed, worldwide allocation was not in the law. Harry Grubert, in a conversation on July 5, 2012, indicated that worldwide allocation would be appropriate.

Option B Version	Income in countries with taxes less than half the U.S. rate (17.5%) are subject to U.S. tax, unless there is an active trade or business. A higher rate encompasses more countries, including Ireland. However, it also has an incentive for affected firms to move income to slightly higher tax rate countries and involves complications in measuring effective tax rates. The provision excepts firms that are making a substantial contribution to a business, a more easily avoided rule than the one in the Discussion Draft which allows an exception only for production for the home market.
Plus Part of Option C	Would also tax royalties at 17.5%, which could in some cases encourage income to be received as royalties. It would encourage exploitation of intangibles abroad and might violate the WTO.

Source: CRS analysis of proposals.

The Ways and Means Discussion Draft addresses the shifting due to leveraging by restricting interest deductions. They impose the lesser of two restrictions. The first is an allocation of interest based on worldwide interest and assets, much like the Grubert and Mutti approach. The second is a limit on interest relative to modified income, and since the limit is not spelled out, the extent of that restriction is yet to be determined. If a high enough ratio of interest to modified income is allowed then the interest allocation would not be very effective and since modified income is prior to not only interest but depreciation and some other production expenses, the ratio would have to be relatively low to be broadly effective. The effectiveness would need to be explored once a percentage is determined. The value of this alternative is not readily apparent given that the first restriction, the allocation rule, provides a reasonable method. The Enzi bill has no interest allocation provisions.

A specific base erosion provision outside of interest has not been chosen in the discussion draft, and it is difficult to determine how effective the base erosion proposals are likely to be. Both Options A and Option B hinge on being in a low tax country and the tax rate is relatively low, only 10%. Option A, which phases out the U.S. taxation of excess intangibles between 10% and 15% may only partially affect Ireland, for example, which has a statutory tax rate of 12.5% and Option B would miss it altogether. These tax rates are effective rates, which is appropriate, but which could be difficult to measure.[81] Options A and C require the identification of intangible income, which is not necessary for B; this problem has been identified as an important complicating factor in several comments.[82]

By triggering current taxation of intangibles when the return exceeds 150% of costs, Option A provides an incentive to push deductible development and marketing costs into the CFC, a point made in Ways and Means hearing.[83] Once a firm falls into the excess profit class a dollar of cost moved to the CFC will decrease income subject to U.S. taxation by $1.50, while increasing taxable income in the United States by $1.00 (although if the tax code retained the production activities deduction and income were eligible for it, this additional dollar would increase taxable income by $0.91).

---

[81] This measurement problem is pointed out by Harrington, Subcommittee on Select Revenue Measures, Ways and Means Committee, November 27, 2011, testimony of John L. Harrington, at http://waysandmeans.house.gov/UploadedFiles/Harringtonsrm1117.pdf.

[82] This complication of Options A and C is pointed out by Stephen Shay and Paul Oosterhuis, KPMG, Will the U.S. Shift to a Territorial System: A Discussion of Chairman Camp's Territorial Tax Draft, at http://www.us.kpmg.com/microsite/taxnewsflash/Corporate/2011/tgi-exec-sum-territorial-tax.pdf and by Michael Reilly, discussion reported in Shamik Trivedi, "Agreement on Territorial Plans Unlikely Despite Commonalities," Tax Notes, February 20, 2012, pp. 949-950.

[83] Subcommittee on Select Revenue Measures, Ways and Means Committee, November 27, 2011, Testimony of T. Timothy Tuerff, at http://waysandmeans.house.gov/UploadedFiles/Tuerffsrm1117.pdf.

Option B, which triggers full U.S. taxation of some income in countries with tax rates below 10% would create incentives to move profits to countries with tax rates higher than the 10% level but lower than the U.S. 25% level. Ireland is a possibility, but there are many potential locations which might not currently be used as tax havens which would become so, including a number of former eastern block countries. It is also possible that jurisdictions that cater largely to U.S. multinationals would raise their own taxes to prevent U.S. firms from leaving. In either case, total U.S. income (the sum of taxes and company profits) would be reduced because a third party (the other countries) would collect a higher share of U.S. firms profits. Option B also is formulated as a cliff: once the country reaches a trigger level all income is subject to full U.S. taxes. Option B exempts from inclusion income derived in the home country (an active trade or business with income derived from the sale of property for use in the country or services provided in the country). These rules may be exploited by firms to avoid the tax.

The drawbacks of option B could also potentially affect option A as well. Since the lower taxes would apply to profits equal to 150% of costs, the lower taxes paid in countries with rates below 10% on this portion of profits would have to be traded off against higher taxes on the excess profits. However, in countries where the costs are small relative to profits firms might also have incentives in this case to shift locations.

Option C, which applies this system only to intangibles and is not triggered by a specific tax rate would also have the merit of not inducing undesirable behavioral changes. Option C would also apply this lower tax to royalties, although at least one analysis has suggested that a lower tax rate on royalties might violate WTO rules on export subsidies.[84] Several critics have pointed out the complication of measuring intangible income which would be a drawback. However, it would still require the measurement of affected income, adding complexity.

The purpose of option B could be accomplished is a way that does not encourage these undesirable behavioral responses by imposing a minimum (combined U.S. and foreign) tax on all foreign source income. Consider, for example, the 60% share of income taxed that comprises the second half of Option C. If a 15% minimum tax were imposed, it would only affect income in those countries with effective tax rates of below 15% but it would not produce incentives to move to a higher tax country.

Option B does appear to have relatively effective provisions defining an active operation that can avoid the tax in the Ways and Means Discussion Draft, although whether companies could work around them remains to be seen. The Enzi bill has a weaker rule, which would might more easily allow firms to justify an exception to the tax authorities and to the courts. The Enzi bill provision is triggered by a higher tax rate, which should capture Ireland.

One witness at the Ways and Means Hearing also noted that there is no distinction in the Discussion Draft between intangibles created in the United States and in other foreign countries: any intangible income could trigger a U.S. tax even if developed outside the United States.[85]

---

[84] Kristen A. Parillo, "Camp Plan Would Likely Violate WTO Rules, Buckley Says," *Tax Notes*, December 12, 2011, pp. 1327-1328.

[85] Subcommittee on Select Revenue Measures, Ways and Means Committee, November 27, 2011, testimony of David G. Noren, at http://waysandmeans.house.gov/UploadedFiles/Norensrm1117.pdf.

Option C of the Ways and Means Discussion Draft and S. 2091 also contains a reduced tax rate for royalties. Under Option C, royalties would be taxed at the same rate as intangible income generated inside the CFC which would eliminate the incentive to shift newly taxed royalties into tax exempt CFC income. If two thirds of royalties were exempt before due to sheltering by foreign tax credits, this change would be a slight relative tax increase (since 40% is taxed), but if the share is lower due to small excess credits and elimination of the splitter rules it could be a tax cut. Similar points could be made about S. 2091.

Transition

The Grubert-Mutti proposal appears to exempt dividends regardless of their source, a view that is probably consistent with their emphasis on reducing tax complexity, such as planning around repatriation. This approach provides a windfall benefit. However, as the Grubert and Mutti study is a general outline, the authors may simply not have addressed transition issues. One of the authors has indicated that it would be appropriate to impose a lower tax on the accumulated unrepatriated earnings in an approach similar to the Ways and Means Discussion Draft.[86]

The Ways and Means Discussion Draft would tax all accumulated earnings before implementation of the reform, but with an 85% exclusion, which may or may not provide a windfall since it might largely apply to earnings that would probably never be repatriated. These earnings would not have to be actually repatriated, but could be deemed repatriated, a benefit that is important if these funds are tied up in illiquid investments. Taxes would be offset by a proportional share of foreign tax credits. In a steady state, most accumulated earnings, based on past evidence and new view theory would be earnings that are permanently reinvested. However, since earnings may have accumulated at higher rates through anticipation of another repatriation holiday, more of these earnings may be planned for distribution.

One critic suggests that the deemed repatriation provision which is extended to individuals as well may not be appropriate for taxpayers not eligible for the dividend exemption.[87] Another suggests that firms may have trouble measuring the total amount of unrepatriated earnings.[88]

S. 2091 has a repatriation tax that differs from the Ways and Means provision in that it is elective on a CFC by CFC basis, the exclusion is smaller at a 70% exclusion and no foreign tax credits would be allowed. However, for income that is not elected to be taxed, the dividend relief would not occur until these accumulated earnings are exhausted. Since firms might eventually wish to repatriate earnings, this rule should create an incentive to repatriate, however, the elective aspect allows firms not to repatriate if their conditions are such that a move of this nature would be difficult (i.e., lack of funds to pay the tax).

---

[86] Conversation with Harry Grubert, July 2, 2012.

[87] Subcommittee on Select Revenue Measures, Ways and Means Committee, November 27, 2011, testimony of John L. Harrington, at http://waysandmeans.house.gov/UploadedFiles/Harringtonsrm1117.pdf. He notes that the purpose may be able to deal with individuals transferring their earnings to corporate form, but suggests that should be dealt with in a more targeted fashion.

[88] Subcommittee on Select Revenue Measures, Ways and Means Committee, November 27, 2011, testimony of Paul W. Oosterhuis, at http://waysandmeans.house.gov/UploadedFiles/Oosterhuissrm1117.pdf.

Current tax treatment is governed in some respects by tax treaties and these treaties may now come into conflict with the new proposed rules. Interactions with treaties would need to be addressed.

An issue to be determined is the treatment of foreign tax credits and losses that have been carried over. For the Grubert-Mutti proposal and the Ways and Means Discussion Draft, which are aimed at a full break from the old system, it seems appropriate to allow foreign tax credit carryovers to lapse (if any foreign tax credit carryovers remain after the taxation of accumulated earnings). That is apparently the intent of the deemed repatriation tax.[89] S. 2091 would presumably continue carryovers for entities not covered (such as branches) and tax credits associated with accumulated income not yet taxed. Treatment of losses under the Discussion Draft has not been addressed, but presumably would continue under S. 2091 which continues aspects of the pre-existing system.

Administrative and Technical Issues

Many of the major rules discussed above would complicate tax administration. The Grubert-Mutti proposal appears to involve the least amount of complication as it has a simple exclusion, somewhat reduces the scope of Subpart F, and has a straightforward anti-abuse provision in the form of the allocation of deductions. There is no scope for a repatriation tax. Although the Ways and Means Discussion Draft is not fully fleshed out, it retains a small repatriation tax that could lead to tax planning (the 5% inclusion of dividend income), and its anti-abuse provisions could be quite complicated. S. 2091 could also potentially lead to a continued repatriation incentive.

This section addresses some other specific issues that have technical and administrative implications.

Including Branches

Including branch company income under the territorial rules is contained in two of the proposals, Grubert and Mutti and the Ways and Means Discussion Draft, but not in S. 2091. There is a good reason for including branches in the scope of the territorial tax, since, if branch income is not allowed or if firms can opt out, then firms could continue to use branches versus subsidiaries for tax planning, to allow the recognition of losses but not positive earnings. Moreover, while there are non-tax reasons for operating as a branch, including branches would equalize the treatment of branch and subsidiary operations.

Nevertheless, one comment suggests that the approach in the Discussion Draft, which treats branches as if they are CFC's subject to all of the other provisions of the proposal comes with additional complications. It is difficult to: measure income of an entity that does not legally exist as if it were separate, determine when a foreign branch exists as designed in the proposal, determine the formation or liquidation of an operation that is not a separate entity, and address the rules that apply to intra-company payments. In addition, firms might shift to operating as a partnership. This comment suggests that branch income simply be exempt from the tax without defining them as CFCs[90] Another comment raises a number of specific tax issues that need to be

---

[89] See comment of Ray Beeman , KPMG, Will the U.S. Shift to a Territorial System: A Discussion of Chairman Camp's Territorial Tax Draft, at http://www.us.kpmg.com/microsite/taxnewsflash/Corporate/2011/tgi-exec-sum-territorial-tax.pdf.

[90] Subcommittee on Select Revenue Measures, Ways and Means Committee, November 27, 2011, testimony of John L. (continued...)

addressed when branches are included, including whether taxes will be triggered by reorganization and the treatment of inter-branch payments.[91]

10/50 Election

The Grubert Mutti proposal includes 10/50 corporations in their exemption system, while the Ways and Means Discussion Draft and S. 2091 allow it as an election. (Recall that a 10/50 company is one where the corporation has a 10% or more share but the company is not controlled by five or less 10% U.S. shareholders). Presumably companies would prefer to elect the exempt treatment especially as they will lose the foreign tax credits associated with dividends. One comment suggested that 10/50 corporations that wish to elect inclusion may have difficulties because they will become subject to Subpart F rules but may not be able to obtain the information on Subpart F income because they do not control the firm. In addition, 10/50 firms may not be able to compel the cash dividend payments needed to pay tax given the tax on accumulated earnings under the Ways and Means Discussion Draft,[92] and may not be able to determine the size of those accumulated earnings.[93] A concern was also expressed that the tax on accumulated deferrals would include income generated before the taxpayer purchased shares in the company.[94] In S. 2091, a similar argument could be made about the elective repatriation, which these firms may not be able to take advantage of.

Foreign Tax Credit Revisions

The Ways and Means Discussion Draft eliminates foreign tax credits for CFC's, branches, and 10/50 corporations except for those associated with Subpart F income. It also eliminates the foreign tax credit baskets, splitter rules, and allocation of indirect expenses to foreign source income (including interest allocation rules). One comment suggests that these changes are problematic because individuals will still be eligible for foreign tax credits.[95] Another adds that these changes in the foreign tax credit would encourage countries to reinstate foreign withholding tax and abrogate treaties because the changes effectively eliminate the limits of current law that credits are limited to foreign source income.[96]

(...continued)

Harrington, at http://waysandmeans.house.gov/UploadedFiles/Harringtonsrm1117.pdf.

[91] Subcommittee on Select Revenue Measures, Ways and Means Committee, November 27, 2011, testimony of T. Timothy Tuerff, at http://waysandmeans.house.gov/UploadedFiles/Tuerffsrm1117.pdf.

[92] Subcommittee on Select Revenue Measures, Ways and Means Committee, November 27, 2011, testimony of John L. Harrington, at http://waysandmeans.house.gov/UploadedFiles/Harringtonsrm1117.pdf .

[93] Subcommittee on Select Revenue Measures, Ways and Means Committee, November 27, 2011, , testimony of Paul W. Oosterhuis, at http://waysandmeans.house.gov/UploadedFiles/Oosterhuissrm1117.pdf.

[94] Report on comment of Jose Murillo at an Ernst and Young Conference, Kristen A. Parillo and Marie Sapirie, "Territorial Plan Drafters Aware of Transition Concerns," *Tax Notes*, November 14, 2011, pp. 810-812.

[95] Subcommittee on Select Revenue Measures, Ways and Means Committee, November 27, 2011, testimony of John L. Harrington, at http://waysandmeans.house.gov/UploadedFiles/Harringtonsrm1117.pdf.

[96] Kristen A. Parillo, "Camp Plan Would Dramatically Affect Withholding, Buckley Says" *Tax Notes*, November 21, 2011, pp. 948-949, reporting comments by John Buckley.

Thin Capitalization Rules and Interest Allocation

One comment raised the question of whether strengthened thin capitalization rules that limit debt would be extended to U.S. subsidiaries of foreign parents (where presumably weaker rules already apply), or at least that intentions in this area might need to be made clear.[97] Although the legislation is focused on U.S. multinationals and their foreign operations, profit shifting can also occur across foreign parents and their U.S. subsidiaries, the current focus of thin capitalization rules.

Another comment pointed out that with more restrictive interest allocation rules firms might want to shift borrowing abroad so that interest could be deducted in other jurisdictions, but that this change might increase borrowing costs.[98] One option that might be considered is to allow loans from the parent to foreign subsidiaries at the borrowing rate of the parent or allow the parent to guarantee subsidiary loans without triggering effective dividends.

Continuing Subpart F

Some discussion of the treatment of the existing anti-abuse rules under Subpart F has occurred. At least one commentator questions why Subpart F, which was developed as a general anti-deferral provision, should continue as is with respect to certain types of income, when income is now generally exempt. One example is foreign to foreign base company income relating to sales and services, which is active income.[99]

Grubert and Mutti suggest that Subpart F should be retained to address profit shifting but modified by eliminating taxes on dividends and also on deemed dividends from investments in the United States. The Ways and Means Discussion Draft makes these two changes although they do not account for the 5% inclusion in income for either. They indicate a further consideration of Subpart F will be made. Grubert and Mutti suggest that the case for other rules such as the foreign base company rules relating to sales and services and interest would be strengthened under a territorial tax. Presumably they are referring to income shifted out the United States. S. 2091, however, specifically excludes this income from Subpart F.

Grubert and Mutti prepared their analysis before check-the-box rules (and the look-through rules) that allow CFC's to disregard their related foreign subsidiaries, which have undermined Subpart F, became so important. The Ways and Means Discussion Draft indicates that these issues will be considered separately and S. 2091 would make the look-through rules (as well as the exclusion of active financing income), currently part of extenders and having expired after 2011, permanent One comment suggested that tax reform should address the leakage in Subpart F including check-the-box and the look-through rules[100] At the same time, one of the concerns about check the box

---

[97] Subcommittee on Select Revenue Measures, Ways and Means Committee, November 27, 2011, testimony of John L. Harrington, at http://waysandmeans.house.gov/UploadedFiles/Harringtonsrm1117.pdf.

[98] Subcommittee on Select Revenue Measures, Ways and Means Committee, November 27, 2011, Testimony of T. Timothy Tuerff, at http://waysandmeans.house.gov/UploadedFiles/Tuerffsrm1117.pdf. See also Paul Oosterhuis, , KPGM, Will the U.S. Shift to a Territorial System: A Discussion of Chairman Camp's Territorial Tax Draft, at http://www.us.kpmg.com/microsite/taxnewsflash/Corporate/2011/tgi-exec-sum-territorial-tax.pdf.

[99] Subcommittee on Select Revenue Measures, Ways and Means Committee, November 27, 2011, testimony of John L. Harrington, at http://waysandmeans.house.gov/UploadedFiles/Harringtonsrm1117.pdf.

[100] Kristen A. Parillo, "Camp Plan Would Dramatically Affect Withholding, Buckley Says" Tax Notes, November 21, 2011, pp. 948-949, reporting comments by Jeff Vandervolk.

---

and look through rules is that the result would not be greater U.S. tax collections but an increase in taxes paid to other countries. For example, if a subsidiary's interest payments from loans to its own high tax subsidiary could not longer be disregarded for purposes of Subpart F with an end to these rules, the response could be to no longer make the loan causing additional tax to be collected by the higher tax foreign country. This outcome would not be beneficial for the U.S. overall since it would reduce the sum of U.S. private profits and U.S. taxes. One comment, for example, notes that exemption would cause firms to have every incentive to reduce foreign taxes paid, and broadening of Subpart F rules should not undo that incentive.[101]

A final comment about Subpart F income is that, since this income is deemed repatriated and not actually paid out, there will be an additional tax under the Discussion Draft and S. 2091 on 5% of income when these earnings are actually paid out as dividends.[102] Thus, 5% of income would be subject to double taxation.

Revenue Consequences

The Grubert-Mutti proposal is projected to raise revenue on a permanent basis, although the gain is small, less than 2% of corporate revenues. Both the Ways and Means Discussion Draft and S. 2091 aim to be revenue neutral over the budget horizon. However, both also rely on a one time revenue gain from taxing existing accumulated earnings. Since this gain is transitory, these proposals will lose revenue on a permanent basis. Since the proposals have not been scored, there is no way to determine how large the permanent revenue loss would be, but it is likely to also be small.

Alternatives to a Territorial Tax

As noted in the prior discussion, there are alternatives to a territorial tax that could address issues associated with repatriation and profit shifting as effectively or perhaps more effectively than the territorial tax provisions. These alternatives fall into three main groups: ending deferral and possibly limiting cross-crediting to move closer to a true worldwide system, reforming the existing system in more limited ways, particularly to address profit shifting, and a hybrid between ending deferral and a territorial tax, such as a minimum tax, which would eliminate the repatriation tax trigger. By traditional theory all of these approaches would probably attract capital back to the United States and improve efficiency in the allocation of capital, although they may create a need to further address shifting of headquarters.

These proposals are summarized briefly. Many of them are addressed in more detail in other CRS reports.[103] Note that many of the same issues that arise with a territorial tax would need to be addressed in some cases, such as dealing with the transition, and dealing with operations outside of CFCs.

---

[101] Subcommittee on Select Revenue Measures, Ways and Means Committee, November 27, 2011, testimony of Paul W. Oosterhuis, at http://waysandmeans.house.gov/UploadedFiles/Oosterhuissrm1117.pdf.

[102] Subcommittee on Select Revenue Measures, Ways and Means Committee, November 27, 2011, Testimony of T. Timothy Tuerff, at http://waysandmeans.house.gov/UploadedFiles/Tuerffsrm1117.pdf.

[103] CRS Report RL34115, *Reform of U.S. International Taxation Alternatives*, by Jane G. Gravelle; CRS Report R40623, *Tax Havens International Tax Avoidance and Evasion*, by Jane G. Gravelle.

Ending Deferral

Ending deferral, as shown in **Table 5**, is estimated to raise $18.4 billion in FY2014. A deferral option is also included in the CBO budget options study and is estimated to raise $11.1 billion in revenue in FY2014.[104] The smaller revenue gain may reflect a provision that eliminates the current interest allocation provision for purposes of the foreign tax credit limit. It would tax income of foreign subsidiaries, while allowing foreign tax credits as in current law. Current taxation would eliminate any disincentive to repatriate, and would also reduce the benefits and scope for profit shifting. Cross-crediting would still be available. It would be more consistent with efficient resource allocation, although issues of shifting headquarters might need to be addressed further. As with territorial tax proposals, transition issues would arise which could be addressed in a fashion similar to that in the Ways and Means Discussion Draft. The revision would require the measurement of earnings under U.S. law, which could add complexity, although such measurement would also be needed for most base erosion measures as well. As with the territorial tax, issues would arise in extending the treatment to 10/50 corporations that have a large U.S. shareholder but are not controlled by a group of large U.S. shareholders, since information on earnings may not be available. This change would, however, permit the elimination of Subpart F.

Ending Deferral and Ending Cross-Crediting Via a Per Country Limit

A greater level of taxation and a more effective provision to discourage artificial profit shifting, which would also eliminate disincentives to repatriate, is to combine ending deferral with a per country limit on foreign tax credits, preventing tax haven income from being shielded by foreign tax credits. This proposal is part of S. 727, the Wyden and Coats general tax reform plan, and is combined with a repatriation holiday similar to that enacted in 2004. This provision was estimated to raise $64.3 billion in FY2014 (see **Table 5**). This larger revenue gain aided in the reduction of the corporate tax rate in that bill to 24%. This provision would require country-by-country measures of foreign taxes paid as well as income (focusing on income earned within that country and not adjusting for intercompany dividends). Provisions would need to be enacted to prevent firms from using holding companies to avoid the per country limit and check the box and look through rules would probably need to be revised.

Measures to Modify the Current System: the President's Proposals

The President has made several proposals that address international tax issues.

The FY2013 budget outline contains several revisions which overall would raise $16.8 billion in FY2014. Note that some of these are complex to explain, and are described in more detail in a Treasury Department document.[105]

---

[104] Congressional Budget Office, *Reducing the Deficit Spending and Revenue Options*, March, 2011, p. 186, at http://www.cbo.gov/sites/default/files/cbofiles/ftpdocs/120xx/doc12085/03-10-reducingthedeficit.pdf.

[105] See U.S. Department of Treasury, *General Explanations of the Administration's FY2013 Revenue Proposals*, February 2012, http://www.treasury.gov/resource-center/tax-policy/Documents/General-Explanations-FY2013.pdf.

- Disallowing interest deductions of parent companies to the extent that income is deferred. This provision is similar to the allocation proposal in Grubert and Mutti but confined to interest and affecting deferred income. An earlier tax reform proposal by Chairman Rangel (H.R. 3970 in the 110th Congress, 2007) would have allocated a broader range of deductions, not just interest. This provision would reduce, although not eliminate, the disincentive to repatriate. ($5.9 billion).

- Limiting foreign tax credits available to the same share of total credits as the overall share of income that is repatriated. This approach would limit tax minimization by repatriating income to absorb foreign tax credits. ($5.5 billion).

- Treating excess intangibles profits as U.S. income, the same provision as Option A is the Ways and Means Discussion Draft, although the budget proposal does not specify the magnitude of the cost mark-up. ($2.5 billion). The proposal would also clarify some rules relating to the valuation of intangibles. ($0.1 billion).

- U.S. insurance companies can reduce taxes by purchasing reinsurance from foreign affiliates, with a deduction of the premiums by the U.S. firm but no tax on the income of the foreign affiliate. This provision would disallow these deductions under certain circumstances. ($0.2 billion).

- Stricter limits on interest deductions would apply to U.S. subsidiaries of firms that inverted (moved their headquarters abroad) prior to the anti-inversion rules adopted in 2004. ($0.4 billion).

- Foreign taxes paid in part to receive a benefit (i.e., the firm is paying a tax in a dual capacity) would not be credited unless the income tax is generally imposed on the country's own residents as well as foreign persons. The current rule does not require the tax to be imposed on the country's residents. This provision typically relates to taxes being substituted for royalties in oil producing countries. ($1.0 billion).

- A codification of regulations that impose on a foreign corporation or nonresident alien tax on gain from a partnership interest to the extent the gain reflects property effectively connected with U.S. business. ($0.2 billion).

- A provision to prevent a foreign affiliate from avoiding characterization as a dividend by making the distribution through a related affiliate with limited earnings and profits, causing the distribution to adjust the cost basis of stock rather than create dividend income. ($0.3 billion).

- Preventing foreign tax credits from offsetting tax on the gain from certain types of asset acquisitions. (0.1 billion).

- A provision that prevents the reduction of earnings and profits without the reduction in foreign tax credits that can currently occur in some transactions. ($20 million).

The Administration also presented a framework for tax reform that mentioned five elements: the allocation of interest for deferred income (first bullet point above), a tax on excess intangibles (third bullet point), a minimum tax on foreign source income in low tax countries, disallowing a deduction for the cost of moving abroad and providing a 20% credit for costs of moving an operation from abroad to the United States.[106]

The minimum tax on foreign source income, which would be a potentially important provision, is not discussed in detail. A minimum tax that could be imposed in the framework of an effective territorial system is discussed below.

Partial or Targeted End to Deferral

A variety of more limited ways of reducing or partially eliminating deferral include eliminating deferral for specified tax havens, eliminating deferral in countries with tax rates that are below the U.S. rate by a specified proportion, eliminating deferral for income from the production of goods that are in turn imported into the United States, eliminating deferral for income from the production of goods that are exported to any other country from the foreign location, and requiring a minimum payout share. These provisions would partially achieve the goals of a general elimination of deferral.[107]

Formula Apportionment

Another approach to addressing income shifting, whether in the current system or a revised territorial system, is through formula apportionment. With formula apportionment, income would be allocated to different jurisdictions based on their shares of some combination of sales, assets, and employment. This approach is used by many states in the United States and by the Canadian provinces to allocate corporate income. In the past, a three factor apportionment was used, but some states have moved to a sales based system. Studies have estimated a significant increase in taxes from adopting formula apportionment.[108] The ability of a formula apportionment system to address some of the problems of shifting income becomes problematic with intangible assets which, unlike production income, cannot be allocated based on tangible assets.[109] There is also a problem of coordinating with other countries so that income would not be double-taxed or never taxed.[110]

---

[106] *The President's Framework for Business Tax Reform A Joint Report by the White House and the Department of the Treasury*, February 2012, http://www.treasury.gov/resource-center/tax-policy/Documents/The-Presidents-Framework-for-Business-Tax-Reform-02-22-2012.pdf.

[107] CRS Report R40623, *Tax Havens International Tax Avoidance and Evasion*, by Jane G. Gravelle This reports also discusses a variety of minor changes in rules including foreign tax credit provisions.

[108] Slemrod and Shackleford estimate a 38% revenue increase from an equally weighted three-factor system Douglas Shackelford and Joel Slemrod, "The Revenue Consequences of Using Formula apportionment to Calculate U.S. and Foreign Source Income: A Firm Level Analysis," *International Tax and Public Finance*, vol. 5, no. 1, 1998, pp. 41-57. Clausing and Avi-Yonah estimate a 35% increase in taxes using sales. Kimberly A. Clausing and Reuven A. Avi-Yonah, *Reforming Corporate Taxation in a Global Economy A Proposal to Adopt Formulary Apportionment*, Brookings Institution: The Hamilton Project, Discussion paper 2007-08, June 2007.

[109] These and other issues are discussed by Rosanne Altshuler and Harry Grubert, "Formula Apportionment: Is it Better than the Current System and Are There Better Alternatives?" Oxford University Centre for Business Taxation, Working paper 09/01.

[110] CRS Report R40623, *Tax Havens International Tax Avoidance and Evasion*, by Jane G. Gravelle, for further discussion.

Hybrid Approaches: Minimum Tax, Partial Territorial Tax

Using the basic territorial approach embodied in the Ways and Means Draft Discussion, it would be possible to generate a relatively straightforward hybrid approach, by a modification of Base Erosion Option B to impose a simpler general minimum tax with no exceptions for active trade or business. Such a revision would technically begin with an elimination of deferral and per country foreign tax credit limit. Income, however, would be taxed at a lower tax rate. This approach would avoid the incentives to shift to a slightly higher tax jurisdiction. Moreover, it would be simpler, because it would not require any measure of a specific type of income, would not require a measure of effective tax rate, and would not require a determination of the type of activity to allow an exception. It would use U.S. rules for measurement of income, but would apply a lower statutory rate to taxable income. Foreign tax credits would need to be allowed on a country by country basis. For example, suppose the statutory rate to be applied were half the U.S. rate, or given current rates, 17.5%. In that case any income from a country with an effective tax rate on taxable income at that level (and probably a lower effective rate overall) would not be subject to U.S. tax. Such a tax regime would only affect tax havens and low tax jurisdictions.[111]

An alternative would be to require income to be repatriated (or deemed repatriated) but subject some share of it to U.S. tax and exempt the rest. An appropriate share of foreign tax credits would be disallowed. For example, if half of income is taxed, the system would be 50% a territorial tax and 50% a world wide tax without deferral. Foreign tax credit limits could be allowed on an overall basis or country by country. This approach bears some resemblance to the foreign tax credit pooling proposal in the President's budget except there is no discretion about repatriation.

Comments made on the combining of a minimum tax with a territorial system suggested that the tax rate would be important, with two observers suggesting a rate of 20%, similar to the rate used by Japan, and indicating that a 10% tax rate is too low.[112]

Both of these proposals would have the effect of eliminating the repatriation disincentive as well as reducing the incentive to shift profits (or at least the cost). Unlike proposals to tax this income at full U.S. rates, such a minimum tax is less likely to shift income to other jurisdictions that have higher rates than the United States.

In any proposal aimed at tax havens, there is a possibility that the haven or low tax country would raise its taxes and capture some of the profits. This problem is more significant with a minimum tax that it would be with full elimination of deferral, which would remove the incentive to profit shift altogether. Tax havens attracting other country's firms might be reluctant to raise taxes and it might be possible to deny credits for taxes that are increased for that purpose.

---

[111] A 2000 Treasury Study proposed a similar treatment and also discussed a tax at a low rate without foreign tax credits. See U.S. Department of Treasury, The Deferral of Income Earned Through U.S. Controlled Foreign Corporations, p. 91, at http://www.treasury.gov/resource-center/tax-policy/Documents/subpartf.pdf.

[112] These observations were made by Reuven Avi-Yonah and Edward Kleinbard, reported in Julie Martin, "Minimum Tax on Multinationals," *Tax Notes*, March 19, 2012, pp. 1498-2000.

Appendix. History of International Tax Rules

As this history indicates, most of the proposals made over the years, whether adopted or not, moved not toward a territorial tax and a reduction in taxation of foreign source income, but toward a worldwide tax and increased taxation.

Deferral of tax on income from foreign incorporated subsidiaries dates from the earliest years of the income tax based reflecting legal principles of the time. The earliest income tax allowed a deduction for foreign taxes, which was replaced by an unlimited credit in 1918. In 1921 an overall limit on the foreign tax credit. similar to current law, was adopted. Beginning in 1932, a per country limit was allowed or required, although regulations that sourced income to holding companies allowed firms to achieve overall limits on their own. The per country limit was eliminated in 1976, although income was sorted into passive and active baskets to prevent this type of cross-crediting.

A number of proposals for changing the system were made but were not (or have not yet been) adopted. Eliminating deferral was proposed by President Kennedy and President Carter. The Kennedy proposals led to the anti-abuse rules (Subpart F) that tax passive and easily shifted income currently.

The Burke Hartke proposal in the 1970s would have repealed deferral and allowed a deduction rather than a credit for foreign taxes. A per country limit was proposed by the Reagan Administration as part of the Tax Reform Act of 1986, but the legislation expanded the number of baskets from two to several instead. The baskets were reduced to two again in legislation in 2004. The main consequence according to tax data, was to include income from financial services in the general basket.

Legislative proposals which would have increased taxation of international income by allocating parent company expenses, such as interest, to deferred income and not allowing it as well as allowing overall foreign taxes to be considered Proposals similar to those of President Obama were included in tax reform legislation proposed by then Ways and Means Committee Chairman Rangel in 2007. A predecessor to the Wyden Coats bill was the Wyden Gregg bill in the 111th Congress. International tax provisions are discussed in detail, through 1989, in William P. McClure and Herman B. Bouma, "The Taxation of Foreign Income from 1909 to 1989: How a Tilted Playing Field Developed," *Tax Notes*, June 19, 1989, pp. 1379.

Author Contact Information

Jane G. Gravelle
Senior Specialist in Economic Policy
jgravelle@crs.loc.gov, 7-7829